THE
POLITICS OF DRAMA
IN AUGUSTAN
ENGLAND

Oxford University Press, Amen House, London E.C.4

GLASGOW   NEW YORK   TORONTO   MELBOURNE   WELLINGTON
BOMBAY   CALCUTTA   MADRAS   KARACHI   LAHORE   DACCA
CAPE TOWN   SALISBURY   NAIROBI   IBADAN   ACCRA
KUALA LUMPUR   HONG KONG

THE
POLITICS OF DRAMA
IN AUGUSTAN
ENGLAND

BY

JOHN LOFTIS

**PROFESSOR OF ENGLISH
STANFORD UNIVERSITY**

OXFORD
AT THE CLARENDON PRESS
1963

PRINTED IN GREAT BRITAIN

THIS BOOK IS DEDICATED
TO MY
MOTHER AND FATHER

PREFACE

SOME fifteen years ago I noted, as generations of students had noted before me, the preoccupation of late seventeenth and early eighteenth-century writers with national politics. In my subsequent study I became convinced that this preoccupation was important in determining the distinctive qualities of Augustan literature, in particular of the drama. The major dramatists, Dryden, Otway, Lee, Rowe, Addison, Steele, Gay, and Fielding, wrote political plays; most of the plays produced in the age have at least a latent political dimension. In earlier books, *Steele at Drury Lane* (1952) and *Comedy and Society from Congreve to Fielding* (1959), I have examined specialized aspects of the political theme in the drama; here in a more comprehensive book I complete my study of the subject.

The dates for plays are those on which they were first made public, either in print or on the stage. I follow the early eighteenth-century calendar except that I consider a year as beginning on 1 January. Except in quotations I have modernized titles. In quotations I follow the spelling and capitalization of the first editions or, rarely, of authoritative later editions.

I gratefully acknowledge a number of obligations: to the editor of *The Huntington Library Quarterly* for allowing me to use, in revised form, material previously published in that journal; to Mrs. Linda Brownrigg, Miss Mary Davison, Mr. Scott McMillin, and Mr. David Sofield for research and editorial assistance; to Mrs. Carol Pearson for compiling the index; to Professor Ernest L. Tuveson and the late John Harrington Smith for interpretative insights; to Professor Emmett L. Avery for assistance with eighteenth-century periodicals; to my colleagues Professors Robert W. Ackerman, Richard Foster Jones, George F. Sensabaugh, and Virgil K. Whitaker for wise counsel; and finally to my wife, for research as well as all other kinds of assistance.

J. L.

Stanford, California
April 1963

CONTENTS

I

INTRODUCTION

IN most periods of history, political writing has been relegated to sub-literary ephemera; in the Augustan age it was given, in the work of a group of major writers, the dignity of high literary form. Swift, Addison, Steele, Rowe, Pope, and Gay, among others, were party writers, and not merely with their left hands. Literature then was immersed in political controversy, a fact that contributes to its distinctive merits—its clarity, wit, and force—as well as to its limitations. If it is less remarkable than the literature of the preceding age for memorable statements of profound experience, the reason is in part the preoccupation with politics that usurped much of the best literary talent. The forceful expression given to partisan views has associated liabilities and assets: as liabilities the particularity of theme and the allusiveness to bygone events which limit the literature's relevance to the concerns of later readers; as assets the vigour and immediacy which go with deeply felt political debate.

More perhaps than any other literary form, drama felt the impress of national politics. Theatres are sensitive at any time to political currents because they depend on public favour; and the theatres of the Augustan age, in which ladies wore face patches according to patterns determined by party (so Addison would have us believe), were emphatically no exception. Contemporary allusions leave little doubt about the violence of party feeling expressed in the theatres. Addison described in the *Freeholder*, No. 34 (16 April 1716), the excess of zeal audiences exhibited for the new king: 'the whole Neighbourhood of the *Drury-lane* Theater very often shakes with the Loyalty of the Audience.' Lewis Theobald described in the *Censor*, No. 93 (25 May 1717), the war of Whig and Tory carried on in the playhouses by way of claps and hisses over the meaning of single sentences. The political rivalry expressed in the applause for *Cato* (1713) is well known, and it appears that such rivalry was not uncommon—if not often so vehement. The reception of *Lady Jane Gray* (1715) was marked by 'Party Claps';[1] and such openly political plays as *The Cobbler of Preston* (1716), *The Non-Juror* (1717), and *The Beggar's Opera* (1728) as a matter of course attracted party approbation or censure. With, I suspect, more truth than scholars have been accustomed to credit him, Cibber attributed the decade-long campaign of abuse that Mist's *Weekly Journal* conducted against him to resentment of the political doctrine of *The Non-Juror*.[2] Certainly the success of that play came from the timeliness of its theme rather than from dramatic merit. The fate of the play in fact illustrates the justice of the complaints that critics judged according to party.[3] Such complaints were frequent and persistent, occurring as late as the middle of the eighteenth century.[4]

Party leaders recognized the value of the theatres as organs of propaganda, in touch with the small group that was dominant politically; and at their bidding playwrights and actors became the spokesmen of faction—notoriously so during the 1730's, when the extravagancies of Fielding precipitated the Licensing Act. Fielding was extreme, but many of the managers and dramatists exhibited discernible political biases that were reflected in the plays they produced or wrote and that were reflected also in the comment they attracted in party-dominated newspapers. The theatres were, to a degree, political institutions; and their managerial policies, including their choice of plays, were influenced by political considerations. Allegiance to theatres on the part of dramatists, like allegiance to friends, often though not invariably followed party lines. Prologues and epilogues, by whomever written, became vehicles for party sentiment, and they attracted a vigorous response from the audience.

At the beginning of Queen Anne's reign John Dennis described, with his unique combination of bias, acerbity, and

---

[1] Allardyce Nicoll, *A History of Early Eighteenth Century Drama*, 3rd ed. (Cambridge, 1952), p. 18.

[2] *An Apology for the Life of Mr. Colley Cibber*, ed. Robert W. Lowe (London, 1889), ii. 186–89.

[3] Cf. *A Vindication of the Press* (1718), reprinted by The Augustan Reprint Society (Los Angeles, 1951), p. 18: 'The Question first ask'd is, whether an Author is a Whig or a Tory. . . .'

[4] Cf. *An Essay on the New Species of Writing Founded by Mr. Fielding* (London, 1751), p. 8.

acuity, the consequences for the drama of his contemporaries' preoccupation with politics. 'Now I leave to any one to judge,' he wrote in his *A Large Account of the Taste in Poetry* (1702), 'whether the imaginative faculty of the Soul, must be more exercised in a Reign of Poetry and of Pleasure, or in a Reign of Politicks and of Business.' The concern with politics, he argued, was a principal cause of what he considered a degeneracy of taste in drama. Comparing the favourable conditions for the production of good comedy in Charles II's time with the allegedly poor conditions in his own, he found, among other circumstances, that there had been a reduction in the number of character types suitable for satire:

For all those great and numerous Originals [of Charles's reign] are reduced to one single Coxcomb, and that is the foolish false Politician. For from *Westminster* to *Wapping*, go where you will, the conversation turns upon Politicks. Where-ever you go, you find Atheists and Rakes standing up for the Protestant Religion, Fellows who never saw a Groat in their Lives, vehemently maintaining Property, and People that are in the *Fleet* and the *Kings Bench* upon execution for their Lives, going together by the ears about the Liberty of the Subject. There is not the emptyest Coxcomb in Town, but has got his Politick Shake and his Shrug, and is pretending to wisdom by Gestures, while his Tongue, the surest Index of his Soul, declares him a very Ass. Go among either the Lame or the Blind, and you shall find them intercepting the Plate Fleet, or sending Forces into *Italy*. For all Men are alarmed by the present posture of affairs, because all men believe they are concerned, which universal alarm has reduced those Characters which were so various before, to a dull uniformity.[1]

Hyperbole aside, the accuracy of Dennis's account of the obsession with politics is abundantly corroborated—among other ways by the popularity as butt for satire of the humble person who neglects his own affairs in favour of the nation's. Farquhar's news-mad beau, Addison and Steele's political upholsterer, Charles Johnson's and Fielding's coffee-house politician, Arthur Murphy's adaptation of Fielding's politician— these characters appeared to observers as representatives of a common failing.[2]

[1] *The Critical Works of John Dennis*, ed. Edward Niles Hooker (Baltimore, 1939, 1943), i. 293.
[2] Farquhar, *Sir Harry Wildair*; *Tatler*, Nos. 155, 160, 178; Charles Johnson,

The interest in politics displayed by Englishmen of the late seventeenth and early eighteenth centuries, even if laughable in some of its manifestations, was well motivated: the political controversies turned on issues of high importance. To be sure, political parties did not exist in the modern sense of well-organized entities; and further, the major antithesis between the Whigs and the Tories was complicated by a distinction between the adherents of the Ministry (Court party) and the opposition (Country party).[1] As at any time, the political action of individuals turned on varying combinations of political theory, private interest, and personal friendship. Still there were generalized differences between the Whigs and the Tories that represented theoretical differences on constitutional principle, on church government, and on economic policy. The differences between Whig and Tory represented much more than mere disagreement on matters pertaining to the interest of separate social groups. The differences of opinion on succession, and thus on the relationship between Sovereign and Parliament, which gave rise to the two parties in Charles II's reign, underwent major alterations, on the Tory side particularly.[2] Yet they persisted through the reigns of James II, William III, Anne, and George I, and even into the reign of George II, though after 1688 they no longer coincide neatly with the distinction between Whig and Tory. The dynastic problem, with its constitutional and ecclesiastical corollaries, provides a fundamental theme of English politics in the Augustan age, giving a certain coherence and unity to the multiplicity of issues which mark the rough and tumble of party manœuvrings. The questions raised in 1678 were not finally answered until the middle years of the eighteenth century. In the intervening years people knew that the questions had not been answered; and they accordingly displayed an interest in them which is akin to that of a reader in a narrative.

The Generous Husband; Or, The Coffee House Politician; Fielding, Rape upon Rape (cf. F. H. Dudden, Henry Fielding: His Life, Works, and Times [Oxford, 1952], i. 72 n.); Arthur Murphy, The Upholsterer; Or, What News?

[1] On the structure of the parties, see Charles Bechdolt Realey, The Early Opposition to Sir Robert Walpole: 1720–1727 (Lawrence, Kansas, 1931); and Robert Walcott, Jr., English Politics in the Early Eighteenth Century (Oxford, 1956).

[2] On Tory political theory, see Keith Feiling, A History of the Tory Party, 1640–1714 (Oxford, 1924).

The analogy of interest in a narrative is not inappropriate. As a result of the rapid development of journalism—in the political pamphlet, the periodical essay, and the newspaper— Englishmen of the Augustan age had extensive information on public affairs, foreign and domestic. The humble man obsessed with public affairs, who is the subject of the satiric portraits to which I have referred, has an addiction to newspapers; and by the time of Queen Anne's reign there were a lot of them for him to read. Most were organs of political parties, to be sure, in which the accurate reporting of news was subordinated to a propagandistic purpose; but they nevertheless provided substance for the political debates that were carried on in the coffee-houses.

The hundreds of plays first produced during the Augustan age which survive to us in printed form provide a chronicle remarkable for comprehensiveness and particularity. The drama was still the most popular form of literature, not yet having lost supremacy to the novel; it was voluminous, occasionally of high quality, and nearly always in close touch with the audience to which it was directed. Comedy took that audience as its subject, reflecting within dramatic conventions its social assumptions, which were often at the same time political assumptions. Tragedy took as its ostensible subject the affairs of monarchs, nobles, and generals in remote times and places and avoided literal social comment; but the superficial distance from contemporary concerns notwithstanding, tragedy was in even closer touch with the currents of political thought than comedy. The self-bounded world of tragedy, in which practical conclusions could be made to follow from theoretical premises, offered to the Augustans an attractive area for the exploration of political ideas. Dramatists provided in tragedy a set of illustrations of political propositions, in which partisan assumptions were given the appearance of natural law. Even the dullest of Augustan tragedies convey a certain interest as exercises in political theory, as coherent expositions of opinions that were widely and strongly held. They are in a sense case histories worked up from theories expounded in political treatises. They do not represent original thought on the vexed constitutional issues—the drama is a poor medium for the discovery of truth in speculative areas—but they do record the political convictions by which generations of men lived.

Since the players' visit to Elsinore it has been agreed that the drama provides a comprehensive record of the society which produces it. As we follow later seventeenth-century drama from one decade to the next, watching Stuart royalism give way to Lockeian Whiggism, and as we follow early eighteenth-century drama in its progressive alienation from the Government, we come strangely close to the temper of Augustan life. And we observe the literary continuum in which appeared the famous plays of that age which have a permanent claim on our attention.

II

BACKGROUND:
THE POLITICAL THEMES OF
RESTORATION DRAMA

'THAT a divinity hedged the King was . . . the main argument of Royalist theory,' writes Sir Keith Feiling in an allusion to Shakespeare.[1] It is an argument that becomes understandable today when it is supported by the graceful verses of Dryden in his opera, *Albion and Albanius*, written just before Charles II died, and produced (with alterations) just after.[2] Veneration for an anointed King, contempt for democracy, an association of the Whig party with both democracy and the mid-century wars, contempt for religious enthusiasm and nonconformity: all of this is embodied in Dryden's allegory, which is not the less spirited for all its over-simplification. Like his earlier play *The Duke of Guise*,[3] the opera is a dramatic commentary on the Exclusion controversy initiated by the Popish Plot, this time in an allegorical rendering of British history from the interregnum to the accession of James II. And if it is marked by an indignant contempt for Whiggery and democracy, the tone is lightened by the lyrical depiction of the royal brothers, which conveys some of the emotional nuances of seventeenth-century politics.

A Tory version of Restoration history, *Albion and Albanius* depicts in chronological sequence the great episodes of Charles's reign that had actual or potential constitutional significance: the displacement of commonwealth by monarchy; the Popish Plot and the recrudescence of democratic and puritanical zeal; the exile of the Duke of York; the conciliatory policy conducted by Charles on the advice of Lord Halifax; the Rye House Plot and its abortive conclusion; the triumphal return of the Duke of

---

[1] *A History of the Tory Party*, p. 487.

[2] For discussion of the composition and production of *Albion and Albanius*, see Charles E. Ward, *The Life of John Dryden* (Chapel Hill, N.C., 1961), pp. 329–32.

[3] On which he collaborated with Nathaniel Lee.

York with his bride; and—as a necessary afterthought—the peaceful accession of the Duke of York to the throne. The dramatic conflict that animates the allegory is the conflict inherent in the antithesis between peaceful and benign order, represented by monarchy, and self-seeking and malignant anarchy, represented by democracy and its ecclesiastical counterpart, zeal. Thus the tumult accompanying the Exclusion controversy is treated as a resurgence of the unruly forces that were dominant in the interregnum—though there is allegorical acknowledgement, in the depiction of the Duke of Monmouth's followers, of the monarchical strain in the opposition to the Duke of York. Loyalty to the King, as Dryden envisages the ideal he celebrates, allows no area for disagreement. A mystically conceived royal wisdom would seem to be the chief resource of government: as explicit a conception as we can expect in an opera that is graceful despite a load of controversy and allegory. We can understand why Charles, who attended its rehearsals a short time before his death, should have praised it.

Albion and Albanius is politically explicit as few plays were. Yet nearly all drama of the early years after the Restoration, comedy as well as tragedy, reveals a royalist bias. The two theatres, under the control respectively of Thomas Killigrew and Sir William D'Avenant, were adjuncts of the Court, places of recreation for the King and his retinue. Charles II had a knowledge of and taste in the drama—French and to some extent Spanish as well as English—uncommon in sovereigns, and he made his preferences known in a manner which the dramatists could not ignore. Even at the end of his life he was giving suggestions to them: to Crowne, for example, who wrote *Sir Courtly Nice* as an adaptation of a Spanish play recommended to him by the King.[1] Dramatists, then, were perforce courtiers, writing with an eye to their master's convictions, which most of them found congenial enough. Dryden alone, of the more important ones, can be accused of having altered his politics with the Restoration; and the charge has little force even against him.[2] Etherege and Wycherley, with Dryden the most

---

[1] John Crowne, *Sir Courtly Nice* (London, 1685), Dedicatory Epistle to the Duke of Ormonde.

[2] On the consistency of Dryden's political thought, see Louis I. Bredvold, *The Intellectual Milieu of John Dryden* (Ann Arbor, 1934).

important writers of comedy, were cavaliers by temperament, the authors of comedies that give artistic permanence to the splendid insouciance of Charles's early years. Their plays reveal the royalist hostility to the King's enemies in the civil wars, above all to the dissenters of the business community who had supported Cromwell. And as comedy is royalist in its tone and its satirical assumptions, so is tragedy in the reverence of its characterizations of sovereigns and noblemen. The heroic play, that remarkable expression of the tragic spirit in the Restoration, is a dramatic form in which the resources of rhetoric are lavished upon the exaltation of royalty. It has been suggested that the form could not outlive Stuart absolutism;[1] we can at least say that it did not.

In the following century, when Walpole's Bill to license the stage made the relation of the Court to the drama a subject of interest, Lord Chesterfield described in a famous speech the political consequences for the Restoration stage of its dependence on King Charles and his favourites. Chesterfield's remarks merit quotation at length, as the opinion—the prejudiced opinion, to be sure—of a well-informed man whose grandfather (Lord Halifax) had been a leading politician in Charles's time:

This has formerly been the case in King Charles the second's days: the playhouse was under a licence, what was the consequence? The playhouse retailed nothing but the politics, the vices and the follies of the court; not to expose them, no, but to recommend them, though it must be granted their politics were often as bad as their vices, and much more pernicious than their other follies. It is true, the court had at that time a great deal of wit, it was then indeed full of men of true wit and great humor; but it was the more dangerous, for the courtiers did then, as thorough-paced courtiers always will do, they sacrificed their honor by making their wit and their humor subservient to the court only; and what made it still more dangerous, no man could appear upon the stage against them. We know that Dryden, the poet-laureat of that reign, always represents the cavaliers as honest, brave, merry fellows, and fine gentlemen; indeed his fine gentleman, as he generally draws him, is an atheistical, lewd, abandoned fellow, which was at that time, it seems, the fashionable character at court; on the other hand he always represents the dissenters as hypocritical, dissembling rogues, or stupid senseless boobies.—

[1] Cf. Merritt Y. Hughes, 'Dryden as a Statist,' *Philological Quarterly*, VI (1927), 335–50.

When the court had a mind to fall out with the Dutch, he wrote his Amboyna, in which he represents the Dutch as a pack of avaricious, cruel, ungrateful rascals:—and when the exclusion bill was moved in parliament, he wrote his Duke of Guise, in which those who were for preserving and securing the religion of their country, were exposed under the character of the Duke of Guise and his party, who leagued together for excluding Henry IV. of France from the throne, on the account of his religion. —The city of London too was made to feel the partial and mercenary licentiousness of the stage at that time; for the citizens having at that time, as well as now, a great deal of property, they had a mind to preserve that property, and therefore they opposed some of the arbitrary measures which were then begun, but pursued more openly in the following reign; for which reason they were then always represented upon the stage as a parcel of designing knaves, dissembling hypocrites, griping usurers—and cuckolds into the bargain.[1]

Lord Chesterfield emphasizes the legal aspect of the theatres' dependence on the Court. Charles had modified the traditional pattern of governmental supervision of the stage by the Lord Chamberlain and his subordinates when just after the Restoration he granted theatrical patents to Killigrew and D'Avenant, both cavaliers in background and temperament. The patents, which were royal grants of authority that gave the theatrical companies organized by the two men virtual monopolies of the production of plays, prevented competition that might otherwise have come from theatres of a less royalist complexion. Thus the machinery of government reinforced the dramatists' inclination to depict the temper of their best customers, the courtiers.

In the passage quoted, Chesterfield understandably isolates Dryden for special consideration: his plays express more comprehensively than those of any other dramatist the preoccupations of the Restoration Court. His literary eminence over four decades and his social and political prominence gave his work an unrivalled centrality. Because he was a self-conscious writer, who explained in critical essays the principles by which he wrote, we know much about his theory of drama; and his theory, in turn, has political implications. Occasionally he was

---

[1] *Miscellaneous Works of the Late Philip Dormer Stanhope, Earl of Chesterfield*, ed. M. Maty (London, 1777), Vol. i, Part ii, pp. 237–8.

a propagandist, as in the plays cited by Lord Chesterfield, *Amboyna*[1] and *The Duke of Guise*; more often, he wrote without controversial intent, but because he wrote about affairs of state, even if fictional ones, he revealed political convictions.

The convictions were royalist.[2] He avoided, to be sure, an extreme position on the many issues in dispute; but if his allegiance, in the phrase of Dr. Johnson, 'changed with the nation', he nevertheless exhibited throughout his career a conservative turn of mind. His Toryism and his neoclassicism were alike in encouraging a conception of a properly organized society as a stable hierarchy with well-defined gradations surmounted by a monarch. Neoclassicism has as one of its strongest impulses a generalizing tendency: a tendency to portray characters as representatives of their occupations and their social stations. If literature should portray 'nature', as the theorists insisted, and if nature was conceived to be the harmonious scheme of universals of which creation as we know it is an imperfect expression,[3] then the poet should direct his attention, not to the unusual characters whom we encounter in life, but rather to characters who are fit representatives of the ideal order. The neoclassical doctrine of decorum in characterization, to which Dryden as well as Rymer and Dennis and many others gave attention, demanded that a dramatist endow his characters with qualities appropriate to their rank and that he observe punctiliously the social perquisites of their rank. A king should not be shown suffering indignities, nor could he be a tyrant or a villain. All this rested on the assumption that monarchy was a form of government sanctioned in natural law. 'All crown'd heads by *Poetical right* are *Heroes*', wrote Rymer in *The Tragedies*

---

[1] On this play, see Louis I. Bredvold, 'Political Aspects of Dryden's *Amboyna* and *The Spanish Fryar*', University of Michigan *Studies in Language and Literature*, viii (1932), 119–23.

[2] For discussions of Dryden's political ideas, see Hughes, 'Dryden as a Statist'; Bredvold, *Intellectual Milieu*; Louis Teeter, 'Political Themes in Restoration Tragedy' (unpublished dissertation, Johns Hopkins University, 1936), *passim*; Mildred E. Hartsock, 'Dryden's Plays: A Study in Ideas', in *Seventeenth Century Studies*, 2nd Ser. (Princeton, 1937), pp. 71–176; John Harrington Smith, 'Some Sources of Dryden's Toryism, 1682–84', *Huntington Library Quarterly*, xx (1957), 233–43; John A. Winterbottom, 'The Place of Hobbesian Ideas in Dryden's Tragedies', *Journal of English and Germanic Philology*, lvii (1958), 665–83; Bernard N. Schilling, *Dryden and the Conservative Myth* (New Haven, 1961).

[3] Cf. Louis I. Bredvold, 'The Tendency Toward Platonism in Neoclassical Esthetics', *ELH, A Journal of English Literary History*, i (1934), 91–120.

of the Last Age (1678);[1] and if Dryden sometimes portrays his dramatic sovereigns as something less than heroes, his remarks on the subject in his critical essays reveal that he did so with an uneasy conscience.

In his plays we may detect a tension between the conflicting demands of political conviction and critical precept on the one hand and dramatic necessity on the other.[2] His lawful sovereigns are treated with reverence, but they are not without human failings. In an illuminating discussion of Fletcher, which he included in the preface to his adaptation of Shakespeare's *Troilus and Cressida*, he criticized the dramatist's characterization of sovereigns. Fletcher, he writes,

> *gives neither to* Arbaces, *nor to his King, in the* Maids Tragedy, *the qualities which are sutable to a Monarch: though he may be excus'd a little in the latter; for the King there is not uppermost in the character; 'tis the lover of* Evadne, *who is King only, in a second consideration; and though he be unjust, and has other faults which shall be nameless, yet he is not the Hero of the Play: tis true we finde him a lawfull Prince, (though I never heard of any King that was in* Rhodes), *and therefore Mr.* Rymer's *Criticism stands good; that he should not be shown in so vicious a character.* . . . *Nor is* Valentinian *manag'd much better, for though* Fletcher *has taken his Picture truly, and shown him as he was, an effeminate voluptuous man, yet he has forgotten that he was an Emperor, and has given him none of those Royal marks, which ought to appear in a lawfull Successor of the Throne.*

In this discussion Dryden partially absolves Fletcher for his indecorous portrayal of the king in *The Maid's Tragedy* on the grounds that he is not the hero. The qualification is an important one. Dryden thought that greater latitude was permitted in the characterization of a sovereign who did not have the central role; and in fact, except in *Don Sebastian* (where the king is indeed a hero), his sovereigns are not the central characters.

Montezuma, the title character but not the principal one of *The Indian Emperor*, has a nobility appropriate to his rank and a cruelty appropriate to his race. The nobility, however, appears in his deportment, whereas the cruelty is merely implicit in remarks about human sacrifices. In addition to the steadfast courage—and magnanimity—which he shares with other

[1] *The Critical Works of Thomas Rymer*, ed. Curt A. Zimansky (New Haven, 1956), p. 42.
[2] For an extended discussion of this tension, see Teeter, 'Political Themes in Restoration Tragedy'.

monarchs in heroic plays, he possesses a clarity of mind and a freedom from prejudice that place him in the literary tradition of the rational primitives. His response to the presumptuous religious and political claims of the Spaniards reveals, in its devastating logic, an intelligence uncommon among heroic characters.[1] He is the major dramatic agent by means of which Dryden conveys his English version of the 'black legend' of the Spanish conquest of the New World, the character who criticizes the inconsistencies and hypocrisies in Spanish colonial policy. As the victim of the Inquisitorial zeal and the lust for gold of the Conquistadores, he is tortured on the rack; and he bears his sufferings with exemplary fortitude. To be sure, the fact that he is portrayed as a defenceless sufferer of persecution represents an infringement of neoclassical decorum as it was conceived by the stricter theorists, who would have royal dignity maintained. His sufferings, however, are a necessity of Dryden's plot.

In *Tyrannic Love* Dryden portrayed a despot, whose cruel, arbitrary, and impolitic acts provoke his assassination—treated as just retribution for his sins. But Maximin, the tyrant of Rome, is no lawful sovereign; rather, he is a humbly born upstart who has deposed and killed the legitimate ruler (his wife's brother). To Dryden, this circumstance was of decisive importance, as we may assume from his remarks on a similar situation in Sophocles' *Antigone*. After censuring Fletcher in the preface to *Troilus and Cressida*, Dryden observes by way of contrast that Sophocles in *Antigone*, '*though he represent in Creon a bloody Prince, yet he makes him not a lawful King, but an Usurper, and Antigona her self is the Heroin of the Tragedy*'. In *Tyrannic Love* Porphyrius, Captain of the Praetorian Bands, is the protagonist and Maximin the tyrant the antagonist; the fact that he is of humble origin—emphasized in dialogue—shields Dryden from the imputation of indecorum. Maximin's wife reproaches him with the illegitimacy of his rule (I):

> O do not name the pow'rs divine,
> They never mingled their Decrees with thine.

Dryden assumes the justice of dynastic rights to succession and

---

[1] The characterization of Montezuma is considered by Trusten Wheeler Russell, *Voltaire, Dryden, and Heroic Tragedy* (New York, 1946), pp. 54–56, 78, 153–7.

a correlation between inherited rank and virtue, even if in the pagan world of this tragedy about a Christian martyr he does not insist on the divine right of monarchs.

'Heroique Poesie has alwayes been sacred to Princes and to *Heroes*', Dryden said in his dedication of *The Conquest of Granada* to the Duke of York; and his own heroic plays are indeed celebrations of princely grandeur. In them the aristocratic mode of conceiving political experience appears in exaggerated form: the conception, that is, of the State's dependence on the prowess and magnanimity of nobly born leaders. To be sure, some over-simplification of political issues is inevitable if the dramatic action is to be intelligible and coherent, but much more than the usual over-simplification occurs in the heroic plays, and in particular much greater emphasis on the common people's dependence on a few supremely gifted aristocrats. Without exception, the heroes in the plays prove to be of high birth, even when, as with Almanzor in *The Conquest of Granada*, their parentage is not known in the beginning. The influence of these individuals on national destiny must have been such as to gratify even the ultra-royalist prejudices of the Stuarts.

The political meaning of his plays is to be found as much in the subjects he neglected as in those he treated. He provided none of the studies in royal tyranny so prominent in the drama produced just after his death; none of the heroic portraits of patriots defending their fellow citizens against oppression; none of the celebrations of political liberty for which dramatists of William III's and Anne's reigns—Rowe and Addison, among others—showed a predilection; in short, there is no evidence of those Whiggish themes that were to dominate plays of the early eighteenth century. Dryden depicts the common people as a thoughtless and irresponsible mob; as I have said, his hatred of democracy even in modified form animates *Albion and Albanius*, his allegorical rendering of political theory. He is contemptuous of statecraft and of statesmen—and thus by implication of constitutional procedures. By contrast he cele- brates kingship lavishly, portraying it not as a necessary con- dition to the fulfilment of a social compact, but rather as an awesome state sanctioned in the order of nature. He shows for kings the devotion which Addison a few years later shows for liberty.

If the royalist themes of Dryden's earlier plays may be taken as typifying the political temper of the stage in the 1660's and most of the 1670's, the themes of his later plays are not so generally representative. The last years of Charles's reign were marked by political confusion and upheaval, and Whig arguments are heard in drama fitfully and briefly.[1] Thus Dryden, for all his royalism, produced in 1680 his anti-Catholic (but monarchical) *The Spanish Friar*;[2] and Lee, who was soon to join Dryden in writing Tory propaganda, produced in the same year his *Lucius Junius Brutus*—which is at least Whiggish and may deserve the stronger term 'republican'. Still, we may say confidently that until the Revolution the preponderance of dramatic talent was expended on the Tory side.

The course of Nathaniel Lee's career suggests the confusion of these years. His biographer has emphasized the inconstancy of his politics: his dramatization in successive plays of conflicting attitudes toward the controversial religious and constitutional issues.[3] The movement of his thought is from Whig to Tory, from anti-Catholicism and something very like republicanism to royalism; he represents in much more extreme form the change observable in Dryden's progress from satire on the Catholics in *The Spanish Friar* to defence of the King's position in the nondramatic *Absalom and Achitophel* and the plays *The Duke of Guise* and *Albion and Albanius*. Innuendo in Lee's early plays may or may not have been intended as criticism of Charles's personal failings,[4] but the political audacity of his *Lucius Junius Brutus* is unmistakable. The play was performed only a few times in 1680 before it was silenced '*as an Antimonarchical Play, and wrote when the Nation was in a Ferment of* Whig *and* Tory, *as a Complement to the Former*'.[5] Yet in less than

---

[1] See George W. Whiting, 'The Condition of the London Theaters, 1679–83: A Reflection of the Political Situation', *Modern Philology*, xxv (1927), 195–206; and Whiting, 'Political Satire in London Stage Plays, 1680–83', *Modern Philology*, xxviii (1930), 29–43.

[2] Cf. Bredvold, 'Political Aspects of Dryden's *Amboyna* and *The Spanish Fryar*', loc. cit., pp. 123–32.

[3] R. G. Ham, *Otway and Lee* (New Haven, 1931), pp. 164–73. See also Thomas B. Stroup and Arthur L. Cooke (eds.), *The Works of Nathaniel Lee* (New Brunswick, N.J., 1954, 1955), i. 5.

[4] Cf. Ham's remarks about *Nero* and *Theodosius* in *Otway and Lee*, p. 130.

[5] Charles Gildon, Preface to *The Patriot* (1703). An order of suppression was issued on 11 December 1680 (P.R.O., L.C. 5/144, p. 28; cited by Allardyce

two years Lee collaborated with Dryden in *The Duke of Guise* and in less than three wrote independently a play in defence of the King and the Duke of York, *Constantine the Great.*[1]

That *Lucius Junius Brutus; Father of his Country* should have been silenced by the Lord Chamberlain seems in retrospect less surprising than that it should have been written and acted in the first place, for it is animated by a veneration for constitutional principles almost as vehement as that evident in the plays of Rowe and Dennis, produced after the Revolution. To Lee, as to many generations of Englishmen, the early Romans represented the classic instance of opposition to tyranny, and Lucius Junius Brutus the type of stern and selfless patriot, in whom private emotion was subordinate to considerations of state. It was he who rescued Rome from the tyranny of Tarquinius Superbus and restored equilibrium among the different powers of the State, equilibrium needed (according to Cicero and many seventeenth-century theorists following him)[2] for stability in government. His insistence on legality even in a king's action would have had an inescapable application to the politics of 1680 (III):

> Laws, Rules, and Bounds, prescrib'd for raging Kings,
> Like Banks and Bulwarks for the Mother Seas,
> Tho 'tis impossible they should prevent
> A thousand dayly wracks and nightly ruins,
> Yet help to break those rowling inundations,
> Which else would overflow and drown the World.

It is hard to believe that Lee, writing the speech in which Brutus publicly arraigns Tarquin, could have been unaware of the applicability of some of the charges to Charles; among other crimes, Brutus accuses Tarquin of (II)

> Invading Fundamental Right and Justice,
> Breaking the ancient Customs, Statutes, Laws
> With positive pow'r, and Arbitrary Lust;

Nicoll, *A History of Restoration Drama, 1660–1700*, 4th ed. [Cambridge, 1952] p. 10 n.).

[1] Arthur L. Cooke and Thomas B. Stroup, 'The Political Implications in Lee's *Constantine the Great*', *Journal of English and Germanic Philology*, xlix (1950), 506–15.

[2] For discussion of the theory of 'mixed' government and its background in antiquity, see Zera S. Fink, *The Classical Republicans: An Essay in the Recovery of a Pattern of Thought in Seventeenth Century England* (Evanston, 1945).

> And those Affairs which were before dispatch'd
> In public by the Fathers, now are forc'd
> To his own Palace, there to be determin'd
> As he, and his Portentous Council please.

In direct statement by normative characters and in reverse statement by despicable characters, the play opposes tyrannical absolutism and celebrates the rule of law in a mixed government.

Here, then, a decade before the publication of Locke's *Two Treatises on Government* and a full generation before Addison's *Cato*, there is an assimilation in tragedy of the political principles that became Whig orthodoxy after the Revolution. The hostile contemporary reception notwithstanding, this is a tragedy of high order; perhaps indeed (if such a comparison can have meaning) a better tragedy than the more famous *Cato*, which was produced at as favourable a time for its reception as *Brutus* was at an unfavourable one. Lee, like Addison, employed emphatic, unqualified statement in his characters' enunciation of political opinion, a form of statement that has the rhetorical advantage of seeming to be an enunciation of natural law. His dialogue is less epigrammatic than Addison's and consequently less quotable, but it has the compensating advantage of moving much more rapidly. *Brutus* is a tragedy; *Cato*, as many have said, a dramatic poem. *Brutus* deserves more attention than it has received as an English statement—perhaps the best English dramatic statement—of the influential ideal of Roman political liberty based on an internal balance of powers.

Yet however Whiggish the play, Lee within two years was on the Tory side. We may only assume that, like many other Englishmen, he was alienated from Shaftesbury and the Whigs by the party's excesses in reaction to the alleged Popish Plot.[1]

The Duke of Guise, which Lee and Dryden wrote in collaboration, has major thematic parallels with Dryden's near-contemporary poem *Absalom and Achitophel*. It, too, is propagandistic in its support of the King and his brother in the Exclusion controversy, and it consequently has a more emphatic and explicit ring of royalist politics than Dryden's other plays. The history of sixteenth-century France provides a subject, as it often did in

---

[1] Keith Feiling (*History of the Tory Party*, p. 175) writes that the political tide turned in favour of the Tories about Christmas of 1681.

seventeenth-century England, from which a political moral is
drawn[1]—a moral sufficiently relevant to the current crisis for
its applicability to be inescapable. The dynastic problem of
France late in the sixteenth century was even more strikingly
parallel to that of Restoration England than was the situation
in Israel in King David's time. The claims of the King of
Navarre, the legitimate heir of Henry II of France, were opposed
on religious grounds by a powerful, audacious, and well-
organized faction, which had in the Duke of Guise its own rival
candidate for the succession. Thus Guise in the play, like
Absalom in the poem, becomes an allegorical representation
of the Duke of Monmouth; and indeed Monmouth's con-
spiratorial activities are rendered with more circumstantial
accuracy and greater harshness of judgement in the play than
in Dryden's poem. If the dramatists' depiction of Henry II is
far from idealized, they portray his (and Charles's) cause as
just; and they reveal contempt for the common people and for
the politicians who use the mob's undisciplined force for
seditious ends. The play is a blunt propaganda piece; but it has
some permanent claim on our attention as a dramatic gloss on
Absalom and Achitophel, the finest political satire of the seventeenth
century.

The finest political satire in dramatic form is *Venice Preserved*,
in which Otway achieved a union of politics and pathos un-
equalled in effectiveness in British drama. A tragedy produced
in 1682, in the wake of the turmoil aroused by the Popish Plot,
about an abortive political insurrection and its villainous
leaders—this would not seem to promise a play remarkable for
the intensity and tenderness of the emotions aroused. That it
is remembered not as a propaganda piece (which it is) but rather
as a tragedy of pathetic love is testimony to the adroitness with
which Otway reconciled dissimilar themes. It is not an allegory
of the Popish Plot or of any other English political event, though
two of the characters, Antonio and Renault, represent different
aspects of the career of Shaftesbury, the Whig leader.[2] If we
may judge by the dexterity with which Otway used suggestive

[1] See J. H. M. Salmon, *The French Religious Wars in English Political Thought* (Oxford, 1959).
[2] For detailed analysis of the play, see A. M. Taylor, *Next to Shakespeare: Otway's Venice Preserv'd and The Orphan, and Their History on the London Stage* (Durham, N.C., 1950), pp. 39–72.

political materials, he was at pains to avoid the semblance of political allegory. He focuses attention on the private emotions of the three chief characters, Pierre, Jaffeir, and Belvidera; and he employs the plot against Venice and the counterplot against the conspirators largely as agencies by which to evoke his protagonists' responses. Both the conspirators and the senators may be identified with the Whigs, and both groups are in a measure contemptible. The play has, and was intended to have, a Tory bias. But its subsequent success on the stage with generations to whom Shaftesbury and the Popish Plot represented ill-remembered lessons in history bears witness to its independent vitality.

The play is indeed remarkable in that its political theme remains significant even to a reader or a spectator who has no knowledge of the events, parties, and personalities that provided the occasion for it. The tyranny and corruption of the governing aristocracy lend plausibility to Pierre's and Jaffeir's decisions to join the conspiracy; the corruption of Renault lends conviction to Jaffeir's decision to betray it. The ambiguity of the dramatist's implied attitude toward the conspiracy gives meaning to the dilemma in which Jaffeir finds himself. The reader follows his sequence of judgements on the conspiracy: from uncertainty to sympathy back to uncertainty—and concluding, as Otway intended, with hostility.

The movement of the political theme runs parallel to that of the love theme and prevents the excessive emphasis on it which is a hazard of neoclassical tragedy, with its neat patterns of dramatic action and rhetorical clarity. Love is a part-time—not a full-time—occupation, as the fact of Jaffeir's political entanglements helps to remind us. We are not so reminded in *The Orphan*, Otway's other famous tragedy, by which our attention is likely to be less than fully engaged because the abundant pathos is unrelieved by the play of ideas. In *Venice Preserved* the political theme provides the additional—and saving—dimension. Although the political satire of the play took contemporaries for its mark and was accordingly a source of added piquancy for the first audiences, it could lose its special relevance with the passage of time without destroying the life of the play.

After 1682 the political temper of the theatre as of the nation cooled.[1] Plays with political overtones appeared from time to time, of course, and political notes were sounded in prologues and epilogues. Lee's *Constantine the Great* appeared in November 1683 and carried on the allegorical satire directed at the Whigs and their leader, Shaftesbury (who had died ten months before in Holland, whither he had fled after the Tory triumph). Dryden wrote a jovial epilogue for the play, damning the Whigs and glancing satirically at the Rye House Plot as well as at the Popish Plot:

> They believe not the last Plot, may I be curst,
> If I believe they e're believ'd the first.[2]

Dryden's *Albion and Albanius*, that dramatic summation of the Tory position presented in 1685 at the beginning of James's reign, may well be taken as an index to the political temper of the theatre in the three years preceding the Revolution.

The Government, as I have suggested, had much to do with the royalist temper of the theatres; the stage was always in theory, and often in practice, subject to governmental supervision.[3] The effective restraint on politically minded dramatists came, not from the critics or the public, but from the patentees or from the machinery of stage regulation supervised by the Lord Chamberlain. However, the nature and extent of governmental supervision was ambiguous and variable; there was neither a well-defined theory of supervision nor a well-defined delegation of authority. The Lord Chamberlain and his subordinates, in particular the Master of the Revels, had at least from the time of the Tudors exercised a measure of control over the theatrical companies of London. The Master of the Revels licensed new plays for production, and in granting or refusing a licence acted as a censor. Charles II introduced confusion into the pattern of supervision when he granted the theatrical patents

---

[1] Whiting, 'The Condition of the London Theaters', loc. cit.; and Allardyce Nicoll, 'Political Plays of the Restoration', *Modern Language Review*, xvi (1921), 224–42.

[2] Cf. W. B. Gardner's note in *The Prologues and Epilogues of John Dryden* (New York, 1951), p. 301.

[3] See Nicoll, *Restoration Drama*, pp. 9–10, 284–342; Leslie Hotson, *The Commonwealth and Restoration Stage* (Cambridge, Mass., 1928), pp. 197 ff.; Arthur F. White, 'The Office of Revels and Dramatic Censorship During the Restoration Period', *Western Reserve University Bulletin*, xxxiv (1931), 5–45.

to Killigrew and D'Avenant, in that he failed to define the relationship between the patentees and the Lord Chamberlain; and
almost from the beginning there were misunderstandings and
antagonisms. The papers of Charles's first Master of the Revels,
Sir Henry Herbert, provide a record of jurisdictional disputes
arising from the absence of a definition of the separate authorities.[1]
Despite continuing disputes, however, the patterns of dele-
gated authority were not made clear until 1737, when the
authority of the Lord Chamberlain was strengthened.

Except for attacks on Catholicism, the Whig point of view
seems to have been permitted little expression; and after 1680
anti-Catholicism largely disappears. Censorship became very
active;[2] among the plays suppressed were Lee's *Lucius Junius
Brutus*, Nahum Tate's adaptation of *Richard II*, and Crowne's
adaptation of *Henry VI*, Part I. Shadwell's *The Lancashire Witches*
was permitted only after large parts of it had been struck out;
and even Dryden and Lee's Tory *The Duke of Guise* was delayed
several months. But although the expression of Tory principle
was encouraged by the Government, it often met noisy opposition from the Whigs in the audience.[3] They could not gain
a dramatic hearing for their own views, but they could at least
make it difficult for the audience to hear the actors declaim the
views of the Tories.

Attendance fell off in consequence of the obsession with
politics; and in fact the political upheaval seems to have contributed to the decline in the prosperity of the theatres which
had issue in 1682 in the merger of the two companies into the
single United Company, which went its troubled way for some
thirteen years. Until mid-way in King William's reign, in 1695,

---

[1] Joseph Quincy Adams (ed.), *The Dramatic Records of Sir Henry Herbert* (New
Haven, 1917), pp. 85–89; 101–6; 113–16; 119–23.

[2] Frank Fowell and Frank Palmer, *Censorship in England* (London, 1913),
pp. 102–6; White, 'The Office of Revels', loc. cit., pp. 15–16.

[3] The epilogue of Otway's final play, *The Atheist* (1683), describes the activities
of the Whigs in the audience:

> It is not long since in the Noisie Pit
> Tumultuous Faction sate the Judge of Wit;
> There Knaves applauded what their Blockheads writ.
>   At a Whig-Brother's Play, the Bawling Crowd
> Burst out in Shouts, as zealous, and as loud,
> As when some Member's stout Election-Beer
> Gains the mad Voice of a whole Drunken Shire.

London had only one theatre—Drury Lane—and aspiring dramatists only one market for their wares. It would seem more than fortuitous that this thirteen-year period coincides approximately with the lull in productivity between the two brilliant phases of late seventeenth-century drama.

These thirteen years mark of course a critical period in English history—the death of Charles II in 1685 and the accession of James II, the Revolution of 1688 and the accession of William III. The Revolution brought not only a notable reversal in the political temper of the drama, but also a change in the relation of the Court to the theatre. James had lacked his brother's literary accomplishments as well as his affability, but he too played the role of royal patron. William, however, had less leisure and liking for the drama, and his wife was a pious lady whom much of seventeenth-century drama could not please. She commanded performances of plays with some frequency,[1] to be sure, but she was temperamentally incapable of the enthusiasm for the theatre shown by her uncle.[2]

Once again dramatists depicted royal tyranny and Catholic

[1] As revealed by warrants for payments to the theatre (P.R.O., L.C. 5/149, p. 368; L.C. 5/151, p. 369. Cited in Nicoll, *Restoration Drama*, p. 352).

[2] Characteristically, almost the only anecdote we have of Queen Mary's association with the theatre has as its point her embarrassment by a play. The story goes that, soon after her accession, she commanded a performance of Dryden's *The Spanish Friar*—as in fact theatrical records reveal that she did for 28 May 1689 (P.R.O., L.C. 5/149; cited in Nicoll, *Restoration Drama*, p. 352). The anti-Catholic theme of the sub-plot could no longer give offence, but the dynastic implications of the main plot were not inoffensive to the daughter of James II, for in this plot a daughter succeeds by force to the throne of her father. The Queen had to withstand the stares of the audience, as they looked back from the pit at her in the Royal Box, when lines spoken by the actors could be given a double meaning—as here (IV):

> What generous man can live with that Constraint
> Upon his Soul, to bear, much less to flatter
> A Court like this! can I sooth Tyranny?
> Seem pleas'd to see my Royal Master murther'd,
> His Crown usurp'd, a Distaff in the Throne. . . .

King James had not been murdered, to be sure, but the other circumstances of his misfortune were close enough to those of the stage monarch for a quick-witted audience to seize on them gleefully.

Authority for the anecdote is a letter written—or allegedly written—by Daniel Finch, second Earl of Nottingham. Sir John Dalrymple, who was given a copy of the letter by Thomas Percy, printed it in *Memoirs of Great Britain and Ireland*, 2nd ed. (London, 1773), ii, Appendix to Part the Second, pp. 78–80. The theatrical records for the performance on 28 May 1689 provide corroboration.

atrocity; Jacobites became customary targets of ridicule; Whigs regained prominence in the theatre, as in the nation. To be sure, the drama did not at once become as stridently Whig as in James's reign it had been Tory. Only after Nicholas Rowe's *Tamerlane* of 1701 did dramatization of the constitutional principles which were used to justify the Revolution become a commonplace of tragedy. But by the time Queen Anne succeeded her brother-in-law, the way had been prepared for the eighteenth-century hegemony of Whig ideas on the stage.

The reappearance in the theatre of Dryden's *The Spanish Friar*, in a performance commanded by Queen Mary on 28 May 1689, was a sign of the abrupt change in the official attitude toward Catholicism. And several months later a notable indictment of Catholicism was produced: Lee's *The Massacre of Paris*. It is a horror play, a dramatization of the St. Bartholomew's Day massacre, probably written in 1679 as a contribution to the Protestant propaganda evoked by the Popish Plot.[1] At the request of the French ambassador, it had been forbidden production in Charles's reign; but its propagandistic theme gained rather than lost relevance and was if anything more timely in 1689, several years after the Revocation of the Edict of Nantes and at the beginning of a war between the Catholic and Protestant powers. Drury Lane produced the play handsomely in November, and the Queen honoured it with her presence, a circumstance that would have emphasized its political meaning. It has the simplicity, directness, and emphasis of propaganda; but it has a tragic force uncommon in propaganda, which is after all rarely written by persons as gifted as Lee. From intrigue it progresses to the concluding horror of the atrocities themselves, described though not dramatized, such violent ones as to have made the play unsuitable for representation except when the nation was aroused by a Catholic threat. The play became (as Lee's editors observe) 'the stock offering of the London stage in times of anti-Protestant unrest';[2] it was revived in the aftermath of the Jacobite rebellions of both 1715 and 1745.

The Revolution brought equally abrupt changes in the politics of individual dramatists: of D'Urfey and Crowne, for example, who now wrote Williamite satire as they had earlier

---

[1] Stroup and Cooke, *Works of Lee*, ii. 3.   [2] Ibid.

written royalist.[1] D'Urfey's *Love for Money* (1689) and Crowne's *The English Friar* (1690) both include harsh satirical thrusts at the Jacobites. Against a backdrop of such timeserving, Shadwell and Dryden appear in their separate ways patterns of political integrity: Shadwell as Whig[2] and Dryden as Tory. Their duel in nondramatic satire at the time of the Exclusion controversy is famous, and so is their reversal of roles after the Revolution, when Shadwell, the '*True-Blew-Protestant* Poet,' replaced Dryden as Poet Laureate. In the interval between these events, neither had written principally for the stage. After his *The Lancashire Witches* of 1681 Shadwell in fact seems to have found the stage closed to his plays. No other was produced until May 1688, when *The Squire of Alsatia* appeared; and in the dedication to the Earl of Dorset of his *Bury Fair* (1689), Shadwell, exaggerating the length of time involved, attributed his silence to his politics: 'I never could Recant in the worst of Times, when my Ruine was design'd, and my Life was sought, and for near Ten years I was kept from the exercise of that Profession which had afforded me a competent Subsistence.'[3]

As we might expect from the new Poet Laureate, *Bury Fair*, Shadwell's first play produced after the Revolution, contains several political thrusts, including a light-hearted comment in the final scene on non-resistance as 'a Doctrine fit for all Wives, tho for nobody else'. Neither here, however, nor in his next play, *The Amorous Bigot* (1690), is the political strain more than incidental; in the latter play it resides in the satirical treatment of the Irish priest Tegue O Divelly, resurrected from *The Lancashire Witches* to do service again against the Catholics. But in his *The Scourers* (1690), political satire becomes more prominent. The Jacobites are his chief target: their disloyalty to the Government and their foolish hopes from France. Sir Richard Maggot, 'A foolish *Jacobite* Alderman' who is a variant of the familiar merchant stereotype of Restoration comedy,

---

[1] Arthur F. White, 'John Crowne and America', *PMLA*, xxxv (1920), 459–60; Cyrus L. Day (ed.), *The Songs of Thomas D'Urfey* (Cambridge, Mass., 1933), pp. 10–14.

[2] Albert S. Borgman, *Thomas Shadwell: His Life and Comedies* (New York, 1928), pp. 52–74.

[3] According to an anecdote published in *The Muse's Mercury*, January 1707, Dryden, Poet Laureate during the years in question, was partially responsible for Shadwell's exclusion from the stage.

shows his folly in his political aberration. 'Here's to the *Turk*, the *Pope*, and King of *France*,' he exclaims (III), 'we are of one side now.'

Just as the Revolution allowed Shadwell to return to his profession of dramatist, it forced Dryden, by the reduction in his fortunes which came with his loss of Court positions, to turn dramatist again. Since *The Duke of Guise* in 1682, he had produced for the stage only *Albion and Albanius*, so preoccupied had he been with his great nondramatic poems of the 1680's. Thus it was as an indirect consequence of the Revolution that he wrote in 1689 one of his best plays, *Don Sebastian*, in which his twin alliances to neoclassicism and royalism appear in harmonious conjunction. The title character is his idealized portrait of the magnanimous sovereign, not an awesome and invulnerable figure, however, but a victim of an unfortunate love and for a time a captive, who nevertheless retains the ability to compel devotion. Generous and dignified even in affliction, he represents in his bearing the qualities appropriate to his rank. In the most celebrated scene of the play, he reduces the hatred of his former subject and present jailer to total loyalty. In this exchange between Don Sebastian and Dorax, the concept of the divinity of kings appears as an inevitable and controlling one, forcing itself upon the unwilling mind of Dorax, who comes at last to acknowledge the inalienable claim of his sovereign to his loyalty.[1] Produced as it was in 1689, the play could scarcely have failed to put some of its first audiences in mind of their inalienable duty to their unfortunate sovereign, James II. Dryden understandably took care to protect himself from the imputation of having written a seditious play by dedicating it to the Earl of Leicester, brother of the Whig martyr Algernon Sidney.

Dryden was bolder in his *Cleomenes, the Spartan Hero* (1692). The annalist Narcissus Luttrell's comment, under the date 9 April 1692, is blunt and to the point:

> By order of the queen, the lord chamberlain has sent an order to the playhouse prohibiting the acting Mr. Drydens play called the tragedy of Cleomenes, reflecting much on the government.[2]

---

[1] Act IV. For detailed discussion of other possible political references in *Don Sebastian*, see John Robert Moore, 'Political Allusions in Dryden's Later Plays,' *PMLA*, lxxiii (1958), 36–42.

[2] *Brief Historical Relation of State Affairs* (Oxford, 1857), ii. 413.

Notwithstanding this order, the play was soon afterwards produced, thanks to the assistance Dryden received from Laurence
Hyde, Earl of Rochester, and his family. Dryden dedicated the
play to Rochester (the uncle of the Queen), thanking him for
'Redeeming this Play from the Persecution of my Enemies', and
explaining at length how the Earl and his daughter-in-law had
championed it. As defensive measures, Dryden stated in his
preface that his plan for the tragedy had its origin seven or
eight years before (and thus prior to the Revolution); and he
prefixed to it a biography of Cleomenes translated from Plutarch
by Thomas Creech—this to demonstrate that details to which
exception had been taken were present in the classical original.

The Lord Chamberlain took no exception to any part of the
play, Dryden says in the preface (though the more cautious
players removed some passages): ' 'Tis printed as it was acted;
and I dare assure you, that here is no Parallel to be found: 'Tis
neither Compliment, nor Satyr; but a plain Story, more strictly
followed than any which has appear'd upon the Stage.' Perhaps so—but he and everyone else who saw or read it must have
understood that the situation of the Spartan King Cleomenes,
in exile and hopeful of assistance from a foreign prince in accom-
plishing his restoration, bore a resemblance to that of King
James in France. James would have understood the poignancy
of Cleomenes' opening soliloquy (1):

> .   .   .   .   .
> I fled; and yet I languish not in Exile;
> But here in *Egypt*, whet my Blunted Horns;
> And meditate new Fights, and chew my Loss.
> Ah! why ye Gods, must *Cleomenes* wait
> On this Effeminate Luxurious Court,
> For tardy helps of base Egyptian Bands?

Small wonder that Dryden needed the intercession of the Queen's
uncle to gain permission for the play to be produced. This was
no tragedy for a politically timorous man to write.

The theatrical monopoly of the United Company was broken
in 1695 by the actors' revolt led by Thomas Betterton. For complaints which seem to have been well founded, Betterton and
other leading actors gained the sympathy of the Earl of Dorset,[1]

---

[1] Brice Harris, *Charles Sackville, Sixth Earl of Dorset, Patron and Poet of the Restoration*
(Urbana, 1940), pp. 129–31.

then the Lord Chamberlain, and of Sir Robert Howard, the old Whig dramatist and politician, and through them gained an audience with the King himself (who seems to have been curious to see the celebrated actors).[1] Although Christopher Rich operated Drury Lane under authority of both patents that Charles II had granted to Killigrew and D'Avenant, the King granted the actors a royal licence which enabled them to open, in April 1695, a new theatre in Lincoln's Inn Fields. Thus was established the theatrical situation that persisted through much of the early eighteenth century, with two theatres competing with one another and contending for Court favour.

Although Lincoln's Inn Fields enjoyed certain marks of Court favour,[2] it cannot be said that the plays presented there were more favourable to the régime than those presented at Drury Lane. To be sure, the most vociferous Williamite play, *Tamerlane*, was presented at Lincoln's Inn Fields, and the theatre attracted the patronage of the Whig Kit-Cat club;[3] it is also true that the only Jacobite play of the period, Bevill Higgons's *The Generous Conqueror*, was presented at Drury Lane. Yet examining the corpus of plays presented at each theatre, we do not discover differences in political coloration such as developed in George I's reign. It seems that nearly all dramatists supported the Court party's (and the King's) military policies. They admire soldiers; scorn the militia; scorn civilian profiteers who are ungrateful to soldiers; bitterly resent the poverty to which disbanded soldiers were reduced by the demobilization enforced by Parliament following the Treaty of Ryswick in 1697; and approve the military preparations that preceded the War of the Spanish Succession. Several of the dramatists were officers (Dilke, Vanbrugh, Farquhar, and Steele), and the audiences would have contained a liberal sprinkling of military uniforms. The dramatists express attitudes that we may assume were common to the soldiers.

Vanbrugh introduces into the first part of his *Aesop* (1696 or 1697) a bumptious squire by means of whom he can satirize the Country party's opposition to the four-shilling land tax; and

---

[1] John Downes, *Roscius Anglicanus, or, an Historical Review of the Stage* (London, 1708), p. 43; Cibber, *Apology*, i. 192–3.

[2] Cf. Cibber, *Apology*, i. 194; ii. 17–19; and *A Comparison between the Two Stages: A Late Restoration Book of the Theatre*, ed. Staring B. Wells (Princeton, 1942), p. 7.

[3] See below, pp. 40–41.

in the second part (1697) he laughs slyly at the claims made for
the militia. In *The Provoked Wife* (1697) he draws a humorous
parallel between a husband's violation of his marriage and King
James's of his coronation vows; and he includes several jibes
at political absolutism. Farquhar's plays are more topical than
Vanbrugh's—more allusive, in particular, to the army and the
wars. The prologue to *Love and a Bottle* (1698) alludes to Farquhar's new commission; and the play itself includes bitter
reflections on the nation's ingratitude to the soldiers. Thinking
of turning soldier, a young gallant meets a cripple, a beggar
who was formerly a soldier, who thus explains his plight (1):

> Our [the beggars'] greatest Benefactors, the brave Officers, are
> all disbanded, and must now turn Beggars like my self; and so, Times
> are very hard, Sir.

This in the year the Tory majority in Parliament, led by Robert
Harley, forced a drastic reduction in the size of the army.[1]
Again, in his *The Constant Couple* (1699), Farquhar sounds a protest against the nation's ingratitude to the army. 'This very
morning, in *Hide Park*,' says Standard (1), a colonel home from
Flanders, 'my brave Regiment, a thousand Men that look'd like
Lions yesterday, were scatter'd, and look'd as poor and simple
as the Herd of Deer that graz'd beside 'em.' William Burnaby
in *The Reformed Wife* (1700) asserts the nation's ingratitude just
as emphatically. He dramatizes the ironies of the peace in
a conversation between Sir Solomon Empty, a war profiteer
who delights in 'railing against the Court Party', and Freeman,
a poverty-stricken captain just home from three years in Flanders.[2]
Significantly, the prologue of the play includes a compliment to
the Whig Kit-Cats.

As we might expect, the advent of the War of the Spanish
Succession evoked enthusiasm from the dramatists. Prologues
and epilogues sound patriotic appeals; dialogue abounds with
war metaphors. Farquhar's *Sir Harry Wildair*, produced about
1 April 1701, conveys an impression of the state of mind, the
sense of expectation, in London on the eve of the new war.
With his soldier's loyalty to the army (and to the navy),
Farquhar again strikes out at civilian ingratitude to disbanded

---

[1] Feiling, *History of the Tory Party*, p. 327; David Ogg, *England in the Reigns of
James II and William III* (Oxford, 1955), pp. 440–1, 449–50.
[2] Act I.

officers—one of whom, Colonel Standard (also in *The Constant Couple*), is a chief character of the play. Colonel Standard has a brother, a naval captain just home from the recent English cruise to the Baltic in support of the Swedes; and the two of them exemplify bluff English integrity in contrast with the Frenchified foppishness evident in the conduct of other characters. Jibes at the French are frequent, and so are allusions to the French religious refugees then swarming to England. News of the Spanish King's long-expected death throws the naval captain, Fireball, into an ecstasy of excitement (II), and he races off to a coffee-house where officers gather to spread the good news. Clearly, Fireball expresses the militaristic views of the dramatist, as does Sir Harry, the title character, who declares his resolution to sacrifice 'Fashions, Coaches, Wigs, and Vanity, to Horses, Arms, and Equipage, and serve my King in *propria persona*, to promote a vigorous War, if there be occasion' (v).

By the time Steele's *The Funeral* was produced about December of the same year, it was clear that the occasion for the vigorous war had come. As in *Sir Harry Wildair*, a comedy of love intrigue is played out against a backdrop of military life—and of military humour. Less topical than the earlier play, *The Funeral* nevertheless includes leading characters who are veterans of William's earlier campaigns and are ready to follow him again. Like Farquhar (and like Shakespeare), Steele has his joke at recruiting, at the medley of improbable characters which a war makes into an army. He puts laughter aside, however, in the fervent song of devotion to William with which he closes the play. Steele, like his brother officer Farquhar, killed his Frenchmen not in person but by means of a dramatic call to arms.

In these years plays were few indeed which could bear a Jacobite interpretation. The fate of Cibber's adaptation of *Richard III*, produced at Drury Lane in 1700, suggests the current sensitivity to anything that could bear a political double meaning, just as it suggests the eagerness of many to find double meaning. The Master of the Revels, Cibber writes, forbade the performance of the entire first act, explaining 'that the Distresses of King *Henry the Sixth*, who is kill'd by *Richard* in the first Act, would put weak People too much in mind of King *James* then living in *France*; a notable Proof', Cibber adds ironically, 'of his Zeal

for the Government!'[1] Crowne was criticized for a few lines
susceptible of a political interpretation in the prologue of his
The Married Beau (1694):

> For your own sakes shew Poetry esteem,
> Lest barb'rous *Picts* you to all Nations seem,
> And now be both in Wit and War out-done,
> In which we once all Nations far out-shone.

For this meagre offence Crowne felt compelled to do penance
by way of an 'Epistle to the Reader' of the published play, in
which he loudly insisted on his enthusiasm for William's Government.[2] And he took care to provide his next play, *Caligula* (1698),
with a patron whose name would dispel any suspicion of disloyalty: Henry, Earl of Romney, brother of Algernon Sidney
and one of the seven signatories of the invitation to William.
His eulogy of his patron provides occasion for a retrospective
glance at the horrors from which England was saved by the
Revolution. 'In this Play,' he adds, 'I set Tyranny before the
Eyes of the World, and the dreadfull Consequences of lawless
and boundless power.' His *Caligula* is indeed a frightening depiction of political absolutism.

The political sensitivity of those years rendered unusable
many promising subjects for tragedy. A successful dramatist,
says one of the interlocutors of *A Comparison between the Two
Stages* (1702), referring apparently to Southerne, Crowne, or
Congreve,[3]

had the Story of *Edward the Second* recommended to him for a Subject.
The Chronicle of that Reign is the most moving of any in the whole
History of our Kings, and might be finely hightned by a good Poet;
but after he had read the Story, he saw it very improper for these
Times, and said it was impossible to touch such a Subject without
some allusions that wou'd render him Guilty, and so he threw it by.[4]

Bevill Higgons, the author of *The Generous Conqueror; Or, The
Timely Discovery* (1701), was not so prudent, writing about revolutions and dynastic complexities as politically suggestive as the
story of Edward II. This play is the only one produced at
either theatre during the later years of William's reign that can

[1] *Apology*, i. 275–6.
[2] It is in this epistle that he tells of the objections made to his prologue.
[3] Wells (ed.), *A Comparison between the Two Stages*, p. 173 n.
[4] Ibid., pp. 69–70.

be plausibly interpreted as critical of the King and the Revolution.

We may merely speculate on why a play of such political boldness gained production—especially in view of the caution that otherwise marked the activities of the theatres. I would surmise that the prominence of Bevill Higgons's family had something to do with it—in particular, the fact that he was the cousin of George Granville (later made Lord Lansdowne, one of the 'occasional' peers). Himself a Tory and in 1701 an active dramatist, Granville wrote the prologue, and he may well have used his influence to induce Drury Lane to present the play.[1]

Rowe's *Tamerlane* is at the opposite extreme of the political spectrum; it indeed sums up with extravagant emphasis the Whig constitutional position, just as *Albion and Albanius* had summed up the Tory position. An allegorical eulogy of William, it has the simplicity of a narrative song of praise in which the resemblance of Tamerlane's career to William's is sufficiently general to be flattering without becoming embarrassing. Appearing at the end of 1701 and thus just after the war started and just before the King's death, *Tamerlane* is a call to arms. It was intended by its author and was recognized by the spectators to be an allegory of William's struggle against Louis XIV. In his dedicatory epistle (which as a critic complained says more about William than about the nobleman to whom it is addressed),[2] Rowe mentions the parallels between the lives of Tamerlane and the King: 'Several Incidents are alike in their Stories; and there wants nothing to his Majesty but such a deciding Victory, as that by which *Tamerlane* gave Peace to the World.' Appropriately for a play first produced in the opening months of the War of the Spanish Succession, the first act takes place at dawn on the day of a decisive battle between the forces of Bajazet, an absolutist in monarchical principles who has violated treaties and has enlarged his territories at the expense of his neighbouring sovereigns, and the forces of Tamerlane, a constitutional monarch of temperate disposition who understands that his authority derives from a social compact. These two characters, then, represent the French and English Kings, and at least

---

[1] For an account of Granville's career, see Elizabeth Handasyde, *Granville the Polite* (London, 1933).

[2] Wells (ed.), *A Comparison between the Two Stages*, p. 98.

two lesser characters are identifiable: Axalla, a foreign prince and a lieutenant of Tamerlane, with Prince Eugene; and the Grecian Emperor (who does not appear but is often mentioned) with Leopold, the German Emperor.[1] Other identifications may have been intended. In particular, Omar, Tamerlane's resentful and even traitorous officer, would seem to suggest a violent Whig's conception of the Tory leader Danby (by that time the Duke of Leeds).[2] The dramatic action projects an English Whig's wish: that William would promptly defeat the forces of Louis and take him personally a captive.

Apart from its war-inspired Francophobia, in which at that juncture Whig and Tory could after all join, the play dramatizes the Whig constitutional position. Dramatic action is palpably the servant of propaganda as Tamerlane, hot from battle, debates with his captive sovereign Bajazet their rival theories of kingship. Free to acknowledge the human limitations of his kingly office, Tamerlane views himself as but a superior kind of servant to his people. 'If I boast of ought,' he explains to Axalla just before Bajazet is brought to him (II),

> Be it, to have been Heaven's happy Instrument,
> The means of Good to all my Fellow-Creatures;
> This is a King's best Praise.

In the conversation that follows, Bajazet denies any obligation at all except to follow his own ambition; and he taunts Tamerlane in a transparent allusion to William's difficulties with Parliament:

> Unfit for War, thou should'st have liv'd secure
> In lazy Peace, and with debating Senates
> Shar'd a precarious Scepter, sate tamely still,
> And let bold Factions canton out thy Power,
> And wrangle for the Spoils they robb'd thee of.[3]

But Rowe was writing propaganda, not political theory, and consequently a convincing confrontation of political philosophies does not emerge. The French conception of monarchy is

---

[1] Cf. James R. Sutherland (ed.), *Three Plays by Nicholas Rowe* (London, 1929), p. 339.

[2] Cf. Omar's claim (Act IV) to have arranged Tamerlane's advantageous marriage.

[3] In *A Lash for the Laureate* (1718), Rowe is accused of 'spurning at Majesty'. Cited in Sutherland (ed.), *Three Plays*, p. 339.

distorted; for whatever the liabilities of the French theory of absolutism, it represented no such diabolical capriciousness as Rowe would suggest.

Just as constitutional theory is the theme of Tamerlane's conversation with Bajazet, so is the relation of Church and State, toleration of dissent in particular, the theme of Tamerlane's later conversation with an Eastern holy man, a dervish. Locke's *Letter Concerning Toleration* would seem to provide Rowe's text here as the *Two Treatises of Government* provide it for the constitutional statements. Having a holy man's licence to speak freely to his monarch, the dervish chides Tamerlane with lack of zeal in his failure to use his military victories as a means to propagate the Moslem faith. The equation of Moslem and Catholic would have been inescapable to Rowe's first audiences in such an injunction as this (III):

> Go on, and wheresoe'er thy Arms shall prosper,
> Plant there the Prophet's Name: with Sword and Fire,
> Drive out all other Faiths, and let the World
> Confess him only.

The Eastern monarch's reply takes the form of a reasoned defence of religious toleration—in which Locke's ideas are apparent. Tamerlane reminds the dervish that virtuous men, without violating 'Law Divine', may disagree on religious dogma; and using a deistic argument he cites a certain universality in worship (III):

> And (tho' by several Names and Titles worshipp'd)
> Heav'n takes the various Tribute of their Praise;
> Since all agree to own, at least to mean,
> One best, one greatest, only Lord of All.

William's known advocacy of religious toleration gives point to Tamerlane's statement that attempts to coerce men's thoughts are futile:

> . . . to subdue th'unconquerable Mind,
> To make one Reason have the same Effect
> Upon all Apprehensions; to force this,
> Or this Man, just to think, as thou and I do;
> Impossible!

His argument is not confined to theory. Tamerlane has also the sagacity in practical politics to see—and in this, too, Rowe glances at William—that scheming politicians use religious arguments for selfish and secular ends.

The popularity *Tamerlane* enjoyed was a function of the Whig party's strength. It seems indeed to have been frankly accepted as a party play, performed when the Whigs were in the ascendancy and suppressed when they were not. Thus, it was intermittently produced from 1701 until 1710, after which production ceased altogether for the years of St. John's supervision of the stage,[1] only to be resumed with more frequency and regularity than ever after 1714, when the Whigs had once more been restored to power with the accession of George I. The frequency with which the play was performed in the first half of the eighteenth century would suggest that it was a chief vehicle by which Whig—and Lockeian—ideas on constitutional theory and religious toleration were disseminated.

Produced in the first year of the eighteenth century, *Tamerlane* was curiously prophetic of what was to come in tragedy, in which a seemingly endless series of variations on Lockeian political ideas was to be dramatized against a background of remote times and exotic places. The Stuart royalism so eloquently enunciated by Dryden would be heard no more. In so far as Tory principle gained expression in eighteenth-century tragedy, it is scarcely distinguishable from Whiggism. That in 1713 the Tories could claim *Cato* as their own (whatever Addison's political intentions) suggests at once the ideological distance the party had travelled since Dryden's song of praise to the Stuarts in *Albion and Albanius*. If in comedy the Tory social philosophy was to persist through Anne's reign, in tragedy the strong Whig theme was stated fully and clearly before William's death.

---

[1] James Welwood, who wrote a biographical preface to Rowe's translation of Lucan's *Pharsalia* (London, 1718), referred to the Tory suppression of *Tamerlane* (p. xx): 'And since nothing could be more Calculated, for raising in the Minds of the Audience, a true Passion for Liberty, and a just Abhorrence for Slavery; how this Play came to be discouraged, next to a Prohibition, in the latter End of a late Reign, I leave it to others to give a Reason.'

III

QUEEN ANNE'S THEATRES IN GOVERNMENT SERVICE

QUEEN ANNE's theatres were in the midst of the nation's vigorous activity. Political life was closely associated with the life of the theatres. On the one hand we find the Whig Kit-Cats sponsoring the construction of the Haymarket, on the other the Tory leaders Bolingbroke and Lansdowne dispensing theatrical patronage and keeping a close watch on the plays produced. The war, just getting under way when Anne succeeded William, provided a focus for the drama. Plays abound with military characters, whose talk turns to the current campaigns; and more prologues than not include chauvinistic allusions to British victories. The theatres were after all places of recreation alike for high government officials and officers of the army and the navy. Since campaigns were fought only in the summer, war had a seasonal aspect; and soldiers could come home and attend the theatre in the winter, just as though they were contestants in some giant athletic competition. 'Rejoyce ye Beaux', goes a prologue of 1703,

> for now the Season comes
> To hush Bellona, and to Silence Drums.
> The Troops for Winter-quarters now come in,
> And now your brisk Campaigns at home begin.[1]

Given an audience full of soldiers home from successful campaigns, the dramatists could scarcely fail to show enthusiasm for the war, and in fact until about 1709 there was near unanimity of zeal for it in the theatres. Dramatists lost no time in celebrating victories, while maintaining a discreet silence about reversals. I have already mentioned Farquhar's dramatization in *Sir Harry Wildair* of the hopeful excitement with which the news of the Spanish King's death was received in London, and Rowe's allegorical prediction in *Tamerlane* of a great

---

[1] Francis Manning, *All for the Better; Or, The Infallible Cure.*

national victory over King Louis. The first victory in fact
celebrated was that of the Tory hero the Duke of Ormonde at
Vigo in October 1702. Cibber at once dedicated to Ormonde
his *She Would and She Would Not*, produced at Drury Lane
in November, a play ironically appropriate to the occasion
in that it is an unacknowledged adaptation (either directly
or through an intermediary) of a Spanish play by Tirso de
Molina.[1] Tactfully ignoring Ormonde's near failure at Cadiz,
Cibber writes in his dedication of the 'Late happy News from
Vigo' and the enthusiastic response to it in London. 'While
Children prattle Vigo, and the Boom', he asks in his epilogue,
'Is't fit the Mouth of all Mankind, the Stage, be dumb?' In
view of the excitement over Ormonde's spectacular victory,
Cibber's dedication to him would not have implied a Tory
bias. Such forthright Whigs as Nicholas Rowe and Richard
Steele followed his example, Rowe in the spring of 1703 dedi-
cating *The Fair Penitent* to the Duke's wife and Steele in Decem-
ber 1703 dedicating *The Lying Lover* to the Duke himself.[2]

Ormonde's rival Marlborough promptly came into his own
in the theatres. He, his family, and his associate Godolphin
enjoyed a preponderance of theatrical praise as of everything
else in the nation during the first decade of the century. Even
before Blenheim, Joseph Trapp, in dedicating his *Abra-Mule*
(January 1704) to Marlborough's daughter Henrietta (who
had married Godolphin's son), spoke of her family's superlative
service to the nation. In the summer of 1704 came the capture
of Gibraltar and the victory at Blenheim, and prologue and
epilogue writers celebrated the events. 'Conquest Crowns our
Armies, and our Fleet', boasted one of them in the fall of 1704;[3]
and another in the spring of 1705 claimed with some truth that
the nation had done more in one campaign 'Than we in Ages
could perform before'.[4] Rowe dedicated his *Ulysses* (1706) to
Godolphin, praising his service to the nation in conciliating

---

[1] John Loftis, 'Spanish Drama in Neoclassical England', *Comparative Literature*,
xi (1959), 29–34.

[2] Steele had personal, non-political reasons for gratitude to the Duke of Ormonde,
the patron of his infancy (as he put it), who had procured for him his childhood
appointment to the Charterhouse.

[3] John Corey, *The Metamorphosis; Or, The Old Lover Outwitted*, Lincoln's Inn
Fields, September 1704.

[4] Mary Pix, *The Conquest of Spain*, Haymarket, May 1705.

faction. The prologue to Mrs. Pix's *The Adventures in Madrid* (1706) hails Marlborough as King Louis's conqueror and rather pugnaciously insists on his claims to honour. Thomas Baker introduces a handsome compliment to Marlborough into the dialogue of his *The Fine Lady's Airs* (1708), a play that includes among its characters a 'Brigadier Blenheim'.

But the most graceful dramatic compliment to Marlborough came from Addison, who in 1707 turned into an opera the legend of fair Rosamond and her bower, which was situated in the park of the Duke's grand new palace at Woodstock. Dedicated to the Duke's wife, the opera includes an allusion to the victory at Blenheim by means of a dramatized vision that comforts the sleeping King Henry. When the opera was performed at Drury Lane, a plan of the Duke's palace (then under construction) seems to have been displayed on the stage while King Henry dreamed of the future greatness of Woodstock Park. The new theatre in the Haymarket also complimented the Duke in an opera that year, in Granville's revised *The British Enchanters*, and there too a view of the new palace was displayed.[1] Perhaps Vanbrugh, architect of the palace as well as builder of the theatre, had something to do with the production.

Of the grimmer side of the war, we catch only glimpses. Problems of recruiting provide a background for Farquhar's *The Recruiting Officer* (1706), in which allusions to the Mutiny and Impressment Acts occur;[2] and in one of two epilogues printed with John Dennis's *Gibraltar* (1705) there is a jocular allusion to the stern fact of the press gangs:

> Each of you paid a Shilling, that came in,
> Which going out you shall receive again;
> For on the Stairs twelve grim Tar-pawlins stand,
> Who as you pass shall strike you in the Hand,
> Till each is hurried by a lusty Tar,
> From the Fictitious to true Gibraltar.

The play itself contains barrack-room talk about the results of war in London, chiefly about the high tax on wine and its poor quality. The war-time quality of wine is the butt of more comic

---

[1] Richard Hindry Barker, *Mr. Cibber of Drury Lane* (New York, 1939), p. 68; Handasyde, *Granville*, pp. 96–98.   [2] Cf. Acts II, V.

conversation in the anonymous *Injured Love* (1711)—but this
time there is a vivid suggestion of the growing discontent with
the war. The plays about military life which seem most authentic in circumstantial detail are those of Charles Shadwell,
The Fair Quaker of Deal; Or, The Humours of the Navy (1710) and
The Humours of the Army (1713). Shadwell alone made a sustained
and informed effort to dramatize military life and to exploit as
dramatic subject the abrupt clashes of personality engendered
by war service. He served in Portugal himself, and he wrote
with understanding about the small irritations, rivalries, and
resentments that then as now were common to the soldier's
and sailor's life.

The earlier play (produced at Drury Lane during the excitement of the Sacheverell trial)[1] depicts the lusty activities of
officers and men of the Virginia squadron, just ashore in Deal
after an eighteen-month cruise. But more than their exploits, it
is the characters of the men themselves, as individuals and as
naval types, that preoccupy Shadwell, who shared his father's
fondness for the Jonsonian humour. The officers are a study
in contrasts: Commodore Flip, a salt up from the ranks who
is contemptuous of gentlemen officers; Captain Mizen, a fop
commissioned directly from civilian life who intrudes his
affectations into ship's routine; and Lieutenant Easy, in
command of the Marine detachment, jealous that he and his
men receive their due from the Navy. The sailors' talk in the
play sounds an authentic note in its bawdry, practicality,
cynicism at war profiteers, and freedom from chauvinism and
heroics. In *The Humours of the Army* Shadwell tried a variation
of the earlier dramatic formula and only partially succeeded.
This time his locale is Spain, in the English camp near Elvas.
The implausible appearance of several English girls and the
ensuing love intrigue do not prevent a plausible depiction of
campaigning in Spain, where illness causes more trouble than
the enemy. Shadwell again treats the detail of military life,
this time foraging, recruiting, infraction of discipline, and
punishment; and he depicts convincingly the routine and
unheroic preoccupations of soldiers in the field. He reveals no
resentment, no bitterness at the war itself (as we might expect
from a veteran); rather, a reportorial interest in recording the

[1] See Cibber, *Apology*, ii. 94-95.

nature of military life as it was experienced by the obscure men who made up the armies.

In *The Humours of the Army* Shadwell made timely use of a Spanish locale. So also Dennis in *Gibraltar* (1705), a comedy of love intrigue played out against a background of the military action that led to the capture of the famous rock. These plays represent a curious indirect result of the Peninsular campaign: the increased use of Spanish and Portuguese locales and characters and possibly even plots from Spanish plays. Since Elizabethan times, to be sure, dramatists had frequently turned to Spain and its inexhaustible store of dramatic plots, but during Queen Anne's reign the Peninsula received more than the customary interest. I have already alluded to Cibber's *She Would and She Would Not*, an adaptation of a play by Tirso, as well as to Shadwell's and Dennis's plays. And there were others. Mrs. Mary Pix wrote *The Conquest of Spain* (1705) and *The Adventures in Madrid* (1706); Vanbrugh, *The False Friend* (1702), with Spanish characters and locale; and Francis Manning, *All for the Better* (1703), in which appear two Englishmen in a Spanish locale. The work of Mrs. Centlivre suggests that the occasion for the interest in Spain and Portugal was the war. Her *Love at a Venture* (1706) includes a character who falsely assumes the identity of a colonel just home from Portugal, and characters in the play refer to an earlier meeting in Spain. Of more importance, in a series of plays beginning with *The Busy Body* in 1709 she depicted Spanish customs and characters and probably used some unidentified Spanish plots.

The enthusiasm for the war displayed in the theatres during these years was in some measure conventional. But Marlborough and Godolphin, the great war leaders, enjoyed even more favour from the dramatists than patriotism demanded. Political moderates themselves, they led a coalition government, in the beginning with a Tory and at the end with a Whig bias. Dramatic praise of their war policy would not in the first years of the reign have necessarily indicated a party leaning; but from the winter of 1704–5, when we may date the beginning of the 'High Tory vendetta against Marlborough' (in Trevelyan's phrase),[1] enthusiasm for the two men and for the war increasingly implies Whiggism.

[1] *England Under Queen Anne* (London, 1930–34), ii. 7.

The association of drama with the Whig party in these years can in part be explained by the patronage of the Whig politicians. Judging from the dedications of plays, the lords of the Junto, especially Halifax, seem to have been liberal benefactors of the dramatists. Congreve, Gildon, Thomas Baker, and Rowe dedicated plays to Halifax; D'Urfey one to Wharton; and Mrs. Centlivre one to Somers. D'Urfey dedicated his comic opera *Wonders in the Sun* 'To the Right Noble, Honourable and Ingenious Patrons of Poetry, Musick, &c. The Celebrated Society of the Kit-Cat-Club',[1] of which the lords of the Junto were ornaments. There was no comparable display toward the Tory leaders. Ormonde alone attracted dedications—from Cibber, Doggett, Dennis, Rowe, and Steele; and some of these seem to have been occasioned by his military victories.

Much of the Whig patronage came through the agency of the Kit-Cats, that eminent society of poets and politicians formed just before the turn of the century and by 1700 attending the theatre on occasion in a body. Known in the portraits of Sir Godfrey Kneller as well as by their political deeds and literary triumphs, these lords and gentlemen personify for us that union of politics and wit which provides the distinctive tone of the Augustan age. With Congreve, Vanbrugh, Addison, and Steele at their famous dinner meetings, we may be sure that their talk turned often to the drama and to the theatres—and with some important practical results. The Kit-Cats' service to the stage was substantial indeed, including financial assistance in the construction of the Haymarket Theatre. Cibber writes of a subscription raised for the projected Haymarket by 'thirty Persons of Quality', who have been identified as members of the club. The project, he informs us, was undertaken to assist Betterton's company, which until 1705 acted in Lincoln's Inn Fields, and which had not fared well in the competition with Drury Lane.

To recover them, therefore, to their due Estimation, a new Project was form'd of building them a stately Theatre in the *Hay-Market*, by Sir *John Vanburgh*, for which he raised a Subscription of thirty

---

[1] The dedication seems to have been received with a certain playful attention: the copy of the play now in the Huntington Library bears on its flyleaf an 'Imprimatur' signed 'Henrietta Somerset', presumably the sister of the Duke of Beaufort, who was subsequently the wife of the Duke of Grafton.

Persons of Quality, at one hundred Pounds each, in Consideration whereof every Subscriber, for his own Life, was to be admitted to whatever Entertainments should be publickly perform'd there, without farther Payment for his Entrance. Of this Theatre I saw the first Stone laid, on which was inscrib'd *The little Whig*, in Honour to a Lady of extraordinary Beauty, then the celebrated Toast and Pride of that Party.[1]

This was Lady Sunderland, wife of a lord of the Junto and daughter of the Duke of Marlborough.[2] The Kit-Cats availed themselves of their right to free admission at the Haymarket and sat in a section customarily reserved for them.

Behind much of the Whig—and Kit-Cat—patronage looms the attractive figure of Charles Montagu, Earl of Halifax. Ever since his years at Cambridge, when he collaborated with Prior in a playful rejoinder to Dryden's *The Hind and the Panther*, he had been known as an amateur poet; and as his career took its brilliant course he came to be known as a liberal benefactor of professional poets. His reputation with us is tarnished by an anecdote Pope told Joseph Spence that has as its point Halifax's pretending to more wit than he possessed,[3] and certainly there is reason to assume that his social and political prominence caused an exaggeration of his literary gifts. Yet we may be sure that he was a generous friend to poets and dramatists. After his death Dennis referred to him as the recipient of more dedications than any other person of his time.[4] Cibber in his *Apology* wrote with gratitude of him, and in particular of his support in 1707 of a project to revive a group of old plays:

A Proposal therefore was drawn up and addressed to that Noble Lord for his Approbation and Assistance to raise a public Subscription for Reviving Three Plays of the best Authors, with the full Strength of the Company. . . . This Subscription his Lordship so zealously encouraged, that from his Recommendation chiefly, in a very little time it was compleated.[5]

[1] *Apology*, i. 319–20; Robert J. Allen, 'The Kit-Cat Club and the Theatre', *Review of English Studies*, vii (1931), 56–61.

[2] *Apology*, i. 320 (see note by Lowe).

[3] *Anecdotes*, ed. Samuel Weller Singer (London, 1820), pp. 134–6.

[4] *Remarks on a Play, call'd, The Conscious Lovers, A Comedy* (1723) in Hooker (ed.), *Critical Works*, ii. 251. On Halifax's reputation as a patron, see also *Memoirs of the Life of Charles Montague, Late Earl of Halifax* (London, 1715), pp. 49–50.

[5] *Apology*, ii. 4–5. Joseph Spence referred to Halifax's support of a project which is probably this same one, though he disagreed with Cibber on the date: 'The

The association of the Whigs with the theatre in the earlier years of Anne's reign did not produce any plays notable for political audacity. But political theory, in so far as it was expressed, was dominated by Whig doctrine. Tragedy, more than comedy, proved to be a vehicle by which constitutional principles could be enunciated, and it is to tragedy that we must look at this time for the expression of political ideas in their theoretical aspects. It is worth noting that whereas Whig and Tory had, from Charles II's reign, differed on issues of political theory, they did not fully articulate their differences in social philosophy until the debates over the Treaty of Utrecht. Not until after the Treaty was the Whig espousal of the financial community reflected in the theatre—in sympathetic renderings by Whig dramatists of the traditional character of the merchant. In Anne's reign even such staunch Whigs as Vanbrugh persisted in the depiction of businessmen within a dramatic stereotype not much altered since the early years of the Restoration.[1] When differences in social philosophy did appear, they naturally found their voice in comedy, even as differences in political theory had been heard in tragedy.

Perhaps the most calculated attempt to dramatize political ideology was Dennis's *Liberty Asserted* (1704), a tragedy the Canadian locale and Indian characters of which provide the primitivistic background so useful to theorists. From Dennis's characteristically full preface, we learn much about his intention in writing the play, as well as about the town's reception of it. He wrote it, he explains, to provide emotional support for those principles of liberty in government which John Locke had demonstrated with philosophical cogency; and more specifically to arouse public spirit for an uncompromising opposition to French tyranny. He glances at the growing lack of enthusiasm for the war on the part of the Tories when he explains that his tragedy 'shews a Man who makes a Treaty with the *French* upon private Interest, made by that Treaty the

paper was all in Lord Hallifax's hand writing', Spence wrote, citing Pope as his source of information, 'of a subscription of four hundred guineas for the encouragement of good comedies, and was dated 1709' (*Anecdotes*, ed. Singer, p. 338). Cibber's date seems to be right, for the three plays he specifies were in fact presented at the Haymarket early in 1707 (*Apology*, ii. 5 n.).

[1] See John Loftis, *Comedy and Society from Congreve to Fielding* (Stanford, 1959), Chs. III, IV.

most wretched of Mankind',[1] though he insists that he writes as an Englishman rather than as a Whig. Some of his audience said that the play was Whiggish, and some even that it was republican—both of which allegations he denies, the latter understandably with more vehemence. 'Liberty is Liberty under a limited Monarchy,' he protests with too much vigour for us to doubt that he was a true Whig, 'as much as under a Commonwealth.'[2] At the centre of his dramatic action is a noble Indian who, in his devotion to freedom, persuades the French governor of the province to declare independence from France. The plot has republican implications to counteract which Dennis includes in his last scene (which was omitted in the acted version) an apostrophe to constitutional monarchy, notable for its iteration of Lockeian—and Whig—theory of government. This most successful of Dennis's plays enjoyed eleven performances during its first year, a record that can best be accounted for by the apparent relevance of the French, English, and Indian wars that are its subject to the war which then filled men's minds.

In this play, as in his *Appius and Virginia* of 1709, Dennis uses characters in remote situations to deplore tyranny and to praise political liberty, a practice having the rhetorical advantage of suggesting that what were in fact partisan views had universal application. *Appius and Virginia*, the Whig bias of which is suggested by its dedication to Godolphin at a time when he was under attack from the Tories, follows Livy's famous story of private resistance to public tyranny. Romans to Dennis as to Addison were symbols of noble independence. And lest any one should miss the political theme, Dennis made it explicit at the conclusion of the play in an allusion to the English war.

Other dramatists sounded similar Whig notes. Joseph Trapp in *Abra-Mule* uses Mahomet IV, Emperor of the Turks, as a reluctant witness for constitutional monarchy. 'No Government can e'er be safe', Mahomet says after he has been deposed (v):

> that's founded
> On Lust, on Murder, and Despotick Pow'r.

And Catherine Trotter in *The Revolution of Sweden* (1706) makes

---

[1] *Critical Works*, ed. Hooker, i. 321.   [2] Ibid. 322.

of the Swedes' struggle for independence against Denmark
an historical lesson in the importance of political liberty. However, the most impressive tragic dramatist of the reign, Nicholas
Rowe, did not continue in the Whiggish vein he had opened in
Tamerlane; he rather focused *The Fair Penitent* (1703), *Ulysses*
(1705), *The Royal Convert* (1707), and *Jane Shore* (1714) on
private emotion. To be sure, a passage with dynastic implications in *Jane Shore* gave offence to the Tories and had to be
omitted,[1] but the play has in fact little to do with politics.

The dramatic celebration of political liberty in Anne's
reign comes to its climax in Addison's *Cato* (1713). In its defence
of liberty and opposition to tyranny, the play gives distinguished
statement to political ideas that were already dramatic commonplaces. And in ancestry and by association they were Whig
commonplaces; as already suggested, the fact that the Tories
were compelled by practical considerations to applaud *Cato*
is a measure of the ideological ambiguity of their position.
The emotional impact of the play is suggested by the fact that
it became a favourite with the patriots of the American Revolution. 'What Pity is it', says Cato in anticipation of Nathan
Hale (IV), 'That we can die but once to serve our Country!'
It is significant that the exemplar of the Roman republican
virtues says *country*—not *king* or *emperor*. Roman republicanism
is an awkward companion for Tory royalism.

The fact that political expression in the drama of the earlier
years of Anne's reign is confined to enthusiasm for the war
and dramatizations of political theory is due to the vigilance
of Charles Killigrew, Master of the Revels, who apparently
denied licences to plays outspokenly revealing political attitudes. Charles Gildon, in the preface of his *The Patriot; Or, The
Italian Conspiracy* (1703), provides an informative account of the
censorship in operation. His play, Gildon explains, is an adaptation of Nathaniel Lee's *Lucius Junius Brutus*, which after
several performances in 1680 had been forbidden by the Lord
Chamberlain of the time. In his first revision of the play, Gildon
continues, he removed all of the reflections on monarchy,

---

[1] This passage, 'about the lawfulness/Of *Edward's* Issue' (III), seems to glance at
the story of the Old Pretender's illegitimacy. Cf. Curll's edition of Rowe, *Poems on
Several Occasions* (London, 1714).

though retaining the original protagonist. Killigrew would not license the play. Gildon then changed the setting from Rome to Florence and substituted Cosmo di Medici for Brutus, a substitution made possible by a parallel between their careers. This time Killigrew accepted the play, and it was performed, its prologue disclaiming any anti-monarchical principles.

Early in 1704 Killigrew was commanded by the Lord Chamberlain to be diligent in reading the plays submitted to him.[1] If the evidence of Gildon's experience is typical, it seems unlikely that this was a reprimand; most likely it was occasioned by the moralistic (rather than political) offences of the drama in those years of the Collier controversy. But it is probable that the increased vigilance to which Killigrew was led by the controversy made him even more cautious in treating political innuendo. Where we catch glimpses of him exercising censorship for political reasons, he seems to be sensitive indeed to anything that might give offence to the Government. In a dramatic complaint about the severity of the censorship, a character in Thomas Baker's *Hampstead Heath* (1705) contrasts the freedom of the press with the bondage of the stage. 'Poets now are curb'd in their Performance', observes Smart (1), as he throws away in disgust a book entitled 'Advice to all Parties', 'and harmless Satyr's deem'd offensive Scandal, while factious Monsters scribble downright Mischief, and every Day foment some new Division.'

If the Master of the Revels cast a suspicious eye on plays with political overtones, he was even more firm in refusing to tolerate the dramatic treatment of controversial religious subjects. On the issue of Occasional Conformity, so bitterly debated during the war years, we hear little in the drama. There are at most innuendoes, as in a jibe at hypocrites and latitudinarians in the first act of Thomas Baker's *Hampstead Heath*. In one of the few instances in which we can check Killigrew's deletions in detail, in the surviving manuscript prompt copy of Charles Johnson's tragedy *The Force of Friendship* and his farce *Love in a Chest* (companion pieces of 1710), all reflections on the Church, the clergy, and religion are deleted.[2]

---

[1] P.R.O., L.C. 5/153, p. 434 (cited in Nicoll, *Early Eighteenth Century Drama*, p. 282).

[2] See Edward Niles Hooker, 'Charles Johnson's *The Force of Friendship* and

If, as seems unlikely, we may believe the claim on the title-page of Tom Brown's farce, *The Stage-Beaux Tossed in a Blanket*, a prologue ridiculing Occasional Conformity was spoken at Drury Lane in 1704 by an actor dressed 'half like a *Noncon Parson*, and the other like an *Orthodox Divine*'. But such instances were rare—if indeed they occurred at all. In the comedy of Queen Anne's reign, there seems to be no extended satire directed to a religious subject.

The managerial changes of the middle part of Queen Anne's reign bear testimony alike to the role political influence played in theatrical affairs and to the absence of a clearly formulated governmental policy toward the theatres. The changes were for several years so frequent as to suggest capriciousness on the part of the supervising officials. It was only when the actor-managers took full responsibility for the affairs of Drury Lane in the season of 1711–12 that a measure of stability was restored.

The pattern of theatrical operation that had existed since the actors' revolt of 1695, with Thomas Betterton's company at Lincoln's Inn Fields and Christopher Rich's at Drury Lane, was first altered with the opening in April 1705 of the new Haymarket Theatre, to which Betterton's company transferred.[1] Vanbrugh became its manager along with Congreve, his fellow Kit-Cat dramatist, when Betterton, by now an old man, resigned his leadership, a transfer of authority legally recognized while the Haymarket was under construction when on 14 December 1704 the Queen granted a new theatrical licence.[2]

Soon after the new theatre opened, inadequacies became apparent that were not compensated for by its architectural magnificence. The acoustics, though satisfactory for music, were poor for spoken drama; and the theatre proved to be too far from the places of residence of its patrons.[3] Further, problems of theatrical personnel arose. Congreve quickly had

Love in a Chest: A Note on Tragi-Comedy and Licensing in 1710', *Studies in Philology*, xxxiv (1937), 407–11.

[1] On the Haymarket, see Emmett L. Avery, *The London Stage, 1660–1800*, Part II (Carbondale, Ill., 1960), i. xxvi-xxix.

[2] P.R.O., L.C. 5/154, p. 35 (quoted in Nicoll, *Early Eighteenth Century Drama*, p. 275). [3] Cibber, *Apology*, i. 320–2.

enough of his new post, and before the end of 1705 resigned his share in the management to Vanbrugh,[1] who carried on as best he could until the end of the season (having petitioned the Lord Chamberlain without result to reunite the two companies).[2] During the summer he, too, withdrew from the management when he was able to lease his theatre to Owen Swiney, a former assistant of Christopher Rich at Drury Lane.

Swiney seems to have acted at first as Rich's agent, though the two of them soon quarrelled and severed relations. In the competition between their companies that marked the season of 1706–7, Rich prospered by playing to the town's taste for musical and spectacular entertainments; Swiney suffered, though he had a strong company of actors and presented plays of literary quality. It was at this juncture that Lord Halifax aided Swiney and the Haymarket company by raising a subscription; but more radical help was needed—and it came as the result of a managerial change at Drury Lane.

During the preceding summer of 1706 a former member of Parliament, Colonel Henry Brett, had acquired a large share in the patent of Drury Lane as a virtual gift from one of Rich's silent partners, Sir Thomas Skipwith, who complained that he had received no profit from it.[3] Behind the transfer of the share, according to Cibber, was Skipwith's belief that Brett, 'being a greater Favourite of the People in Power, and (as he believ'd) among the Actors too, than himself was, might think of some Scheme to turn it to Advantage'.[4] In the ensuing winter Brett took over control of the theatre from Rich, who though a minority shareholder had by clever manipulation of his interests long controlled the management. Brett promptly turned to his friends in the Government for aid in reuniting the two theatrical companies: 'he made use of the Intimacy he had with the Vice-Chamberlain', Cibber explains, 'to assist his Scheme of this intended Union, in which he so far prevail'd that it was soon after left to the particular Care of the same Vice-Chamberlain to give him all the Aid and Power necessary

---

[1] John C. Hodges, *William Congreve the Man: A Biography from New Sources* (New York, 1941), p. 77.

[2] L.C. 7/3 (cited in Barker, *Cibber*, p. 62 n. Barker provides a detailed and authoritative discussion of the managerial changes of these years, which serves as a supplement to Cibber's account in his *Apology*).

[3] *Apology*, ii. 31 ff.   [4] Ibid. 32.

to the bringing what he desired to Perfection. The Scheme
was, to have but one Theatre for Plays and another for Operas,
under separate Interests'.[1] Thomas Coke, a Tory member of
Parliament for Derbyshire, had become Vice-Chamberlain
late in 1706; and it is apparent from the surviving letters addressed to him that he was regarded as a potent arbiter of
theatrical affairs.[2]

In January 1708 the theatrical union that Brett desired
was accomplished,[3] a sensible arrangement that ended the
competition by returning all the actors to Drury Lane, where
only legitimate plays were permitted, and by sending the
singers and dancers to the Haymarket, which was thereupon
limited to opera, for which it was much better suited. This
disposition of theatres and personnel, realistic as it was, brought
success to both houses and seems to have been favoured by
everyone but Rich, now reduced from his former dominant
position. When Colonel Brett tired of active participation in
Drury Lane affairs (as he soon did) and turned over his share
in the management to three of the principal actors, Wilks,
Estcourt, and Cibber, Rich reasserted his old authority,[4] but
only until a group of actors apparently led by Cibber gained
the Lord Chamberlain's support in a plot to suppress him. Rich
was evasive in responding to regulatory orders from the Lord
Chamberlain, who in consequence issued an order in June
1709 restraining him from further exercise of the patent.[5] Three
actors, this time Wilks, Doggett, and Cibber, now revealed
that they had entered into articles of agreement with Owen
Swiney and would the following season share the management
of the Haymarket.

In the fall of 1709, when the political temper of the nation was
rapidly turning Tory, a Tory member of Parliament gained a
licence to operate Drury Lane in the place of the silenced Rich.

The Person to whom this new License was granted was *William*

---

[1] *Apology*, ii. 46.

[2] Some of Coke's theatrical papers are now in the Houghton Library of Harvard
University; some of them, in a transcription by James Winston, are in the British
Museum (Add. MS. 38607). There is a report on his papers by The Historical
Manuscript Commission: H.M.C. *Coke* (1889).

[3] Barker, *Cibber*, p. 74.   [4] Ibid., pp. 74–75.

[5] Cibber, *Apology*, ii. 71–73 (see Lowe's note, p. 73, for the order of silence itself).
Barker, *Cibber*, pp. 75–77.

Collier, Esq. [Cibber writes, stressing his connexions with the Court], a Lawyer of an enterprizing Head and a jovial Heart; what sort of Favour he was in with the People then in Power may be judg'd from his being often admitted to partake with them those detach'd Hours of Life when Business was to give way to Pleasure: But this was not all his Merit, he was at the same time a Member of Parliament for *Truro* in *Cornwall*, and we cannot suppose a Person so qualified could be refused such a Trifle as a License to head a broken Company of Actors.[1]

His influence at Court, however, did not assure him of the co-operation of his actors, and during his first season (1709–10) he had a disastrous time with them. Swiney had parallel difficulties with his partners the actor-managers at the Haymarket; and he was quite ready to join Collier in negotiations to which the Lord Chamberlain was a party.[2] It was agreed in November 1710 that Swiney and the actor-managers should lead a company at Drury Lane devoted to legitimate drama, and Collier an operatic company at the Haymarket, Collier to receive the additional benefit of a subsidy of £200 from the other company. The actor-managers soon settled their personal troubles with Swiney by excluding him from an active share in the management and agreeing to pay him £600 a year.[3]

Whether the initial proposal for the next exchange first came from Collier (as Cibber implies)[4] or from Swiney is uncertain, but in any event it was soon decided between them that they should trade theatres, and in April 1712 new licences were issued, recognizing the exchange. Collier thenceforth received the stipend of £600 from the actor-managers and Swiney carried on as best he could with the opera at the Haymarket during the season of 1712–13, until he was compelled by debts to break away and flee to the Continent to escape from his creditors.[5]

The complexities of personal intrigue responsible for this remarkable series of managerial experiments are not relevant here; and, in fact, they are known only in outline—from Vice-Chamberlain Coke's papers, records of litigation, and Cibber's *Apology*. But certain important conclusions are justified.

---

[1] *Apology*, ii. 91–92.   [2] Barker, *Cibber*, pp. 84–85.
[3] Ibid., pp. 85–87.   [4] *Apology*, ii. 107. But cf. Barker, *Cibber*, p. 87.
[5] Ibid. 107–9. Cf. Barker, *Cibber*, p. 87.

The management of the theatres clearly required a highly
specialized skill, and courtiers, regardless of party, lacked the
ability to perform the duties required. Richard Steele, replac-
ing Collier as nominal head of Drury Lane after the accession
of George I, said as much.[1] It was only after the actor-managers
worked out a compromise agreement with Swiney making his
position a sinecure that their management became stable and
efficient. Queen Anne's Ministers apparently thought of the
supervisory posts as Court favours—with the important limitation that the favours could be dispensed only in a manner
consistent with the prosperous operation of the theatres. Patent
rights were only loosely recognized: witness the silencing of
Rich and thus also of other minority shareholders.[2] Court
favour was decisive in determining managerial changes, and
hence national politics had an impact in the theatres: the influence of the Whigs, evidenced in the activities of the Kit-
Cats, gave way after 1709 to an even stronger influence of the
Tories.

The Tory political victory of 1710 had an immediate consequence for the theatres. For the four remaining years of
Queen Anne's reign performances were subjected to an even
more intense scrutiny, by Government and audience alike,
calculated to bring into view real and imagined political
innuendo. Because Ministerial supervision was too severe to
permit more than the mildest criticism of governmental policy,
such expression of party opinion as reached the stage was
mainly Tory; but the Whigs were active in the background,
attempting, even if not often successfully, to gain a hearing.
Before 1710 no high government officials other than the Lord
Chamberlain and his subordinates, the Vice-Chamberlain
and the Master of the Revels, took interest in the routine
operation of the theatres. But when Harley (later Lord Oxford)
and St. John (later Lord Bolingbroke) came to power in that
year, they gave attention to the stage as to all media of public
persuasion. It was to this period that Cibber alluded when he
remarked that the Court 'had now a mind to take the publick

---

[1] In *The Theatre*, No. 7 (1720).

[2] The alleged violation of property rights in the silencing of Rich is the subject
of a petition to the Crown by the various shareholders in the patent, drawn up
about 1709: B.M. Add. MS. 20726, pp. 22–23.

Diversions more absolutely into their own Hands'.[1] A journalist writing a generation later, in *The Daily Gazetteer*, 13 June 1737, stated that Lord Bolingbroke himself—the Secretary of State—exercised the duties of a stage censor:

> In the Tory Part of Queen *Anne*'s Reign, 'tis well known that *Bolingbroke*, the Craftsman's Patron, survey'd all the Plays before they were acted; and, for Example, struck out, as I remember particularly, two Verses in *Rowe*'s *Jane Shore*, because of something in them, tho' remote, that displeas'd them.[2]

This statement is corroborated by what we know of the preliminaries to the production of Addison's *Cato* in 1713: Addison, as we shall see, submitted the play to Bolingbroke before it was performed.[3] The fact that only three or four new plays a year were produced in London would have made it possible for the busy Secretary of State to read all of them.

In supervising the theatres Bolingbroke was aided by the Vice-Chamberlain Thomas Coke, perhaps by William Collier, and by George Granville, who seems to have been active as an intermediary between the Tory Ministry and the actors and dramatists. Himself a dramatist and a poet and a liberal patron of other men of letters,[4] Granville had a role in these years which resembles that of Lord Halifax in the earlier years of the reign, though he was closer to Oxford and Bolingbroke than Halifax had been to Godolphin and Marlborough. Following the Tory victory in the elections of 1710, Granville became Secretary of War. After faithful service to the Ministry, he was raised to the peerage as Baron Lansdowne at the beginning of 1712 when he was one of the twelve whom Oxford persuaded the Queen to ennoble in order to ensure the ratification of the Treaty of Utrecht. Later in the same year he was advanced from his post as Secretary of War to the more important one of Comptroller of the Queen's Household, and he was made a member of the Privy Council. A dramatist in such high places would understandably have seemed a desirable patron to men of the theatre who desired favours from the Government.[5]

---

[1] *Apology*, ii. 78.   [2] See above, p. 44.   [3] See below, pp. 59–60.
[4] For his career, see Handasyde, *Granville the Polite*.
[5] Illustrative of Lansdowne's reputation as a patron is a letter which Barton Booth wrote to him on 16 December 1712, when Booth was seeking admission

It was through Lansdowne that the Tory Ministry extended
an offer of some theatrical post, presumably that of governor of
Drury Lane or of the Haymarket, to Richard Steele, then
one of the most active of the Whig propagandists. Our information about the episode is fragmentary (though it is definite
enough); in order to understand it we are compelled to proceed by inference. A cousin of Steele's wife mentioned the Tory's
offer when some years later he dedicated a sermon to Steele
(while Steele was under suspension from his post at Drury
Lane), extolling him for the virtues recommended in the sermon
—in particular, disinterested regard for the public welfare:

> Consider what an appearance you must make to so elegant and
> generous a gentleman as the Lord Lansdowne, who offered you the
> theatre in your own way, without solicitation, in the last reign, now
> it is torn from you, in spite of the strongest instrument by which
> Power could give it you, in this?[1]

Steele had himself made brief allusion to the offer when in
1715 he addressed a petition to King George (requesting
appointment to the mastership of the Charterhouse); at this
time Steele said merely that he had been offered the direction
of the theatre in the previous reign, because it was known that
he was capable of effecting theatrical reform.[2] And in fact
Steele's reputation as a reformer after his great success with
The Tatler, *The Spectator*, and *The Guardian* would have made
him, in view of his long association with the theatre, a logical
choice for a supervisory post in those years when the stage was
under a continuing attack from moralistic critics. Yet the
offer seems to have been prompted mainly by political considerations—by Oxford's desire to gain Steele's allegiance or at
least his journalistic silence. Steele was on good terms with
Oxford through the summer of 1713 and in fact until that time
had received a pension as gentleman-usher to the late Prince

---

to partnership in the management of Drury Lane: 'I know the Worth, and honour
of the Vice Chamberlain, but not being so well Known to Him, as to your Lordship, I have humbly begg'd of You, to be my Patron, and Advocate to him; and
I am well assur'd, he has ever had a just, and true Regard for your Lordship'
(B.M. Add. MS. 38607, p. 9).

[1] David Scurlock, Dedicatory Epistle prefixed to *Public Virtue the only Preservative
of Liberty and Property* (1720). Quoted from George A. Aitken, *The Life of Richard
Steele* (London, 1889), ii. 246–7.

[2] Blenheim MSS. See Aitken, *Steele*, ii. 76.

George of Denmark (Queen Anne's husband) and had held a minor office in the Government, that of commissioner of stamps. 'When I had the honour of a short conversation with you', Steele wrote to Oxford in June 1713, resigning his commissioner-ship, 'you were pleased not only to signifie to me that I should remain in this Office, but to add that if I would name to you one of more value which would be more commodious to me, you would favour me in it.'[1] Perhaps it was at about this time that Lansdowne made him the offer of the theatrical post. In the fall of the same year Steele began his severe journalistic attacks on the Ministry, thus alienating himself from Oxford and Bolingbroke. Here then is an instance of the Government's use, or attempted use, of a theatrical post as a political bribe or reward for political service. Steele's decision not to accept the offer seems to have been a political one: he was ready enough to become governor of Drury Lane when a year or so later, after the accession of George I, the Whigs offered him the position.

Swift, who in these years acted as a dispenser of Tory literary favours, apparently had nothing to do with the offer to Steele.[2] He tried, though as it proved unsuccessfully, to gain a post for another Whig dramatist, Nicholas Rowe, who, *Tamerlane* notwithstanding, seems to have been eager to serve the Tory Ministry in any profitable capacity at all. If we may credit a widely circulated anecdote, Oxford rudely disappointed Rowe's hopes for political preferment. At Oxford's suggestion, the story goes, Rowe undertook a study of Spanish, preliminary he thought to an appointment in which the language would be useful; but when he reported to the Treasurer that he had learned it, Oxford replied that he could then read *Don Quixote* in the original.[3] It is clear that the Tories had little interest in gaining Rowe's support, whatever his eminence as a tragic

---

[1] *The Correspondence of Richard Steele*, ed. Rae Blanchard (Oxford, 1941), p. 79. For a full examination of the Tory offer to Steele, see John Loftis, *Steele at Drury Lane* (Berkeley and Los Angeles, 1952), pp. 25–33.

[2] Ibid., p. 31.

[3] Cf. Spence, *Anecdotes*, ed. Singer, p. 178. There is, curiously, support for the anecdote in the sale catalogue of Rowe's books: he owned a Spanish dictionary, a Spanish grammar, and a copy of *Don Quixote* in the original. (The sale catalogue is in the British Museum.)

For an account of Rowe's efforts to secure employment, see Sutherland (ed.), *Rowe: Three Plays*, pp. 7–12.

dramatist. Unlike Steele he was not a powerful political journalist.

The Ministry did, however, bar from the stage his dramatization of Whig political principles, *Tamerlane*. 'This Play', wrote Rowe's biographer Dr. James Welwood in 1718, 'came to be discouraged, next to a Prohibition, in the latter End of a late Reign.'[1] After having been performed in most of the seasons from 1704 to April 1710, the play was not seen again in London until 1715. Rowe's new tragedy, *Jane Shore*, was produced in February 1714, but as we have seen only after Bolingbroke had cancelled a passage that displeased him. The slights Rowe suffered from the Tories, however, were to be compensated for by the Whigs, who soon after their accession to power in 1714 rewarded him with a series of lucrative posts, including the Poet Laureateship.

If the Tory leaders tried to induce dramatists to write plays expressing the party bias on current issues, as is doubtful, they had only limited success. The enthusiasm for the war disappeared in the theatres, and as early as the summer of 1710, before the Tory victory in the autumn elections, there was a demonstration on the stage against the Duke of Marlborough; but otherwise little of a positive nature can be associated with the party's programme. The demonstration against Marlborough, as it was reported by a German traveller to England, occurred at the Haymarket on 24 July 1710 and thus some time before his dismissal from all his offices in December 1711. In the evening he went to *The Recruiting Officer*, wrote the German,

On this occasion the actors represented a prodigiously satirical Interscenium, which was not to be found in the printed copy of the play. . . . In this interlude a troop of soldiers came on, singing at the top of their voices an English song which had been made by the army in Flanders about the Duke of Marlborough. In it Prince Eugène is praised for his openhandedness, while Marlborough, on the other hand, is blamed for his avarice, so that every verse ended: 'but Marlborough not a penny'.

The people, who are very bitter against the whole family, even the Duke himself, laughed prodigiously and bandied about monstrous insults, although Marlborough's daughter, the Duchess of Montaigu,

---

[1] Preface to Rowe's translation of Lucan's *Pharsalia* (London, 1718), p. xx.

was herself at the play and was so greatly shamed that she was covered with blushes. . . . When the song was at an end, there was such a clapping and yelling that the actors were unable to proceed for nearly a quarter of an hour.[1]

How different indeed from three years before, when Addison's *Rosamond* had celebrated the Duke's glory!

Mrs. Centlivre ran into trouble at Drury Lane in January 1712 out of enthusiasm for Marlborough. From the preface to the published version of her *The Perplexed Lovers*, we learn something of the care taken by the actor-managers during these years to avoid giving offence to the Tories in power, a care exhibited in this instance by their refusal, as Mrs. Centlivre explains, to use an epilogue that contained a complimentary allusion to Marlborough

without I cou'd get it licens'd, which I cou'd not do that Night [of the first performance], with all the Interest I could make: So that at last the Play was forc'd to conclude without an Epilogue. . . . The next Day I had the Honour to have the Epilogue Licens'd by the Vice-Chamberlain, but by this time there was a Rumour spread about Town, that it was a notorious whiggish Epilogue; and the Person who design'd me the Favour of speaking it, had Letters sent her to forbear, for that there were Parties forming against it, and they advis'd her not to stand the Shock; here was a second Blow greater than the first: The sinking of my Play cut me not half so deep as the Notion I had, that there cou'd be People of this Nation so ungrateful as not to allow a single Compliment to a Man that has done such Wonders for it.

The war-time chauvinism apparent in the play, which several years before would have been the merest commonplace, had become controversial. Mrs. Centlivre did not yield in her devotion to the Whigs, and to the House of Hanover whose claims they supported; and she pointedly dedicated her next play, *The Wonder: A Woman Keeps a Secret* (April 1714), to 'His Serene Highness George Augustus, Electoral Prince of Hanover', who before the year was out assumed a more exalted title.

The actor-managers of Drury Lane, Cibber, Wilks, and Doggett, who thus cautiously conducted their affairs, began their prosperous era with the season of 1711–12 a few months after

---

[1] *London in 1710 from the Travels of Zacharias Conrad von Uffenbach*, trans. and ed. by W. H. Quarrell and Margaret Mare (London, 1934), pp. 138–9. See also Avery, *London Stage*, i. 227.

they had returned to Drury Lane from the Haymarket with their nominal partner, Owen Swiney. We hear little of Swiney at Drury Lane, or of William Collier, who in 1712 replaced him as the partner of the actor-managers, but it is important to remember that they were there, and that they were dependent on the Tory Ministry for their highly remunerative positions. Drury Lane could scarcely have been openly Whig, even had the actor-managers desired it to be, so long as Swiney or Collier retained a share in the management.

As a matter of fact the actor-managers showed little taste for political statements of any kind during the political storms that marked the end of Anne's reign. Both Doggett and Cibber were later conspicuous in their demonstrations of devotion to the Whig cause and the House of Hanover, Doggett in establishing the annual waterman's race on the Thames in celebration of the accession and Cibber in writing several political plays and ultimately a series of bad poems as Poet Laureate; but both they and Wilks (who consistently showed less interest in politics) chose to avoid political entanglements when the outcome of the party rivalries was so dangerously uncertain. Cibber, it is true, writes in his *Apology* of himself and his brother-managers as though they were thorough Whigs in 1713 when *Cato* was produced;[1] but contemporary records do not support this view.[2] Indeed, John Dennis in 1720 chided

---

[1] *Apology*, ii. 130–1.

[2] There is some evidence that Cibber supported the Tories during this interval of their supremacy. A book list at the back of the second edition of Thomas Parnell's *Poems* (1726) contains, in addition to a number of works known to be by Cibber, the following entries: 'The Tell-Tale; or, the invisible Witness. . . . By Mr. *Cibber*' and 'The Secret History of *Arlus* and *Odolphus*, Ministers of State to the Empress of *Grandinsula*: In which are discover'd the labour'd Artifices formerly us'd for the Removal of *Arlus*, and the true Causes of his late Restoration upon the dismission of *Odolphus*, and the *Quinqunvirate*. Humbly offer'd to those good People of *Grandinsula*, who have not yet done wondering why that Princess shou'd change so notable a Ministry. . . . By Mr. *Cibber*.' *The Tell-Tale* need not detain us: it is a conventional love story enlivened by an 'invisible witness'. But *Arlus and Odolphus* is a party pamphlet, expressing Tory bias, the descriptive title of which is a fair indication of its contents. The pamphlet, apparently written just after the Tory election victory in the autumn of 1710, is critical of the war policy of Godolphin and Marlborough, whose motives as well as abilities it questions, and conversely approving of Harley. The attribution of the pamphlet to Cibber in the book list is no sure indication that he wrote it; but it establishes a presumption that he did and his known activities provide no reason for assuming that he might not, in 1710, have supported Harley.

Cibber that he was not, before 1714, distinguished for his service to George: 'I would fain hear of some Proof that he gave of his Zeal for the Protestant Succession, before the King's Accession to the Crown.'[1] Cibber, Wilks, and Doggett no doubt understood that their precarious tenure at Drury Lane depended on their not offending the Ministry, and that the prosperity of the theatre depended on their not offending either the Tory or the Whig half of the nation.

The major political event at Drury Lane in the years just before the Queen's death was, of course, the production of *Cato* in April 1713. Writing twenty-five years after the event, Cibber in his *Apology* regarded *Cato* as a Whig play, which the Tories had, for their selfish political ends, appropriated: 'Although *Cato* seems plainly written upon what are called *Whig* Principles, yet the Torys of that time had Sense enough not to take it as the least Reflection upon their Administration; but, on the contrary, they seem'd to brandish and vaunt their Approbation of every Sentiment in favour of Liberty. . . .'[2] But in 1713 the issue was not so clear.

The political meaning of *Cato* was and is still an enigma. Thus one recent scholar has argued that despite the rather general praise of individual freedom Addison probably had no specific party purpose in mind;[3] whereas another, offering new evidence in the form of a critique of *Cato* written by Lady Mary Wortley Montagu, has argued that many of the lines on liberty were added shortly before the play was produced, with a specifically Whig intent.[4] The relevant evidence is curiously conflicting. Addison was not, I should hazard, entirely disingenuous in the matter. He can scarcely be acquitted, if not of a certain amount of double dealing, then of an extreme degree of caution to avoid giving offence.

The anecdote of the Whigs and the Tories, seated on opposite sides of the playhouse, contending with one another in the

---

[1] Advertisement prefixed to *The Invader of His Country* (London, 1720).

[2] *Apology*, ii. 130.

[3] Clement Ramsland, 'Britons Never Will Be Slaves: A Study in Whig Political Propaganda in the British Theatre, 1700–1742', *Quarterly Journal of Speech*, xxviii (1942), 399. Ramsland's article is based upon his unpublished dissertation: 'Whig Propaganda in the Theatre, 1700–1742' (University of Minnesota, 1940).

[4] Robert M. Halsband, 'Addison's *Cato* and Lady Mary Wortley Montagu', *PMLA*, lxv (1950), 1122–9.

vigour of their applause of lines praising liberty is well known;[1] so, too, is the anecdote of Bolingbroke's public gift of fifty guineas to Booth in recognition of his service to the cause of liberty. Bolingbroke's gesture was matched by a similar one from the actor-managers, who were moved, Cibber would have us believe, by the desire to counter a Tory gift,[2] but also, certainly, by a desire to placate Booth with something less than the full share in the profits of the theatre to which his conspicuous success gave him a claim. The play occasioned a spate of pamphlets, in several of which the alleged political allegory was laboriously glossed.[3] The more literal-minded of the Whigs would have it that Cato, champion of personal freedom and possessor of an unshakeable presence of mind and calm, represented the Duke of Marlborough; whereas the Tories professed to see a resemblance between Caesar the tyrant and Marlborough, who had desired the Captain Generalship for life. Some of the political commentaries were quite specific: Juba was identified with the Emperor of Germany, Syphax with Prince Eugène, and Lucius and Sempronius with Oxford and Bolingbroke (these identifications, of course, by the Whigs). But from all of the debate no consensus emerged. Addison denied that he wrote the play with a partisan intention and neither the Tories nor the Whigs were able to gain general acceptance for their interpretations.

The play itself, despite its theme of political liberty, provides no sure clue to Addison's intention beyond establishing the fact that he had no blatant propagandistic motive. As I have said, in its emphasis on opposition to tyranny, the theme of the play is far more compatible with the traditional position of the Whigs than of the Tories. But the Tory position was changing. It is to external evidence that we must look for enlightenment. Most of the first four acts had been written by 1704 and thus may be presumed to have been in the beginning innocent of any very specific political intention. Probably they

---

[1] Letter of Pope to John Caryll: George Sherburn (ed.), *The Correspondence of Alexander Pope* (Oxford, 1956), i. 174–6. See also George Berkeley's account of the performance: Benjamin Rand (ed.), *Berkeley and Percival* (Cambridge, 1914), pp. 113–14.

[2] *Apology*, ii. 130–3.

[3] A number of the pamphlets are listed in Nicoll, *Early Eighteenth Century Drama*, p. 88 n.

expressed a generalized Whiggism but scarcely anything more. Lady Mary Wortley Montagu's criticism of the play a short time before its production for insufficient emphasis on personal liberty suggests that substantial interpolations were made just before production, for such a criticism of the play in its final form, in which praise of liberty is a steady chant, would be unthinkable. Most of the group who urged Addison to complete the play and allow it to be staged were Whigs, who probably thought of it as propaganda for their party. Lady Mary, a strong Whig, obviously thought of it as a Whig play when she wrote her criticism of it; Steele, an uncompromising Whig, packed Drury Lane with a friendly audience for the first performance; John Hughes, a Whig, engaged to write the fifth act himself before Addison supplied it; and Samuel Garth, another Whig, wrote the epilogue. Pope, on the other hand, who was not associated with either party at the time (though in sympathies rather more Tory than Whig), made a number of alterations in the play and wrote the prologue.

Addison, perhaps without the full knowledge of his Whig friends, took pains to see that the play would not give offence to the Tory Ministers. It could scarcely have been a secret that, less than a fortnight before the play was produced, Addison dined with Swift and Bolingbroke, or that two days later Swift attended a rehearsal.[1] But it might have come as a surprise to such a forthright Whig as Steele that Addison allowed Oxford and Bolingbroke to examine the play before it was acted. This we learn from an anecdote Pope told Spence,[2] which casts doubt upon any unqualified Whig interpretation of the play. Addison brought the play to him, Pope said, and asked for his opinion of it. Pope replied that he should print it but not have it acted —because, although well written, it lacked qualities which would make it theatrically effective. Addison concurred at the time, but later told Pope that some especial friends of his (who must have been Whigs) insisted that the play be produced. Addison requested that Pope show it to Bolingbroke and Oxford and assure them that it was not intended as a political play. The Ministers approved it and it was acted. Addison later,

[1] Swift, *Journal to Stella*, ed. Harold Williams (Oxford, 1948), pp. 651–4.
[2] This anecdote was generously made available to me in its entirety by James M. Osborn, from his collection of Spence's papers.

Pope added ironically, made much of it as a party play and so far departed from his moderation as to write *The Freeholder*.

Addison may have been compelled to show the play to Bolingbroke. Yet it would seem that he wanted it both ways—to please his Whig friends and yet not displease the Tories in power. And he had it both ways. The Stoic doctrine of *Cato* was well calculated to call up in the spectators a fine frenzy of patriotic emotions, not differentiated according to party.

When the Tragedy of *Cato* was first acted [Cibber wrote], let us call to mind the noble Spirit of Patriotism which that Play then infus'd into the Breasts of a free People that crowded to it; with what affecting Force was that most elevated of Human Virtues recommended? Even the false Pretenders to it felt an unwilling Conviction, and made it a Point of Honour to be foremost in their Approbation; and this, too, at a time when the fermented Nation had their different Views of Government. Yet the sublime Sentiments of Liberty in that venerable Character rais'd in every sensible Hearer such conscious Admiration, such compell'd Assent to the Conduct of a suffering Virtue, as even *demanded* two almost irreconcileable Parties to embrace and join in their equal Applauses of it.[1]

Cibber's patent Whiggism here need not obscure the essential truth of his testimony to the effect produced by the play.

Its very success proved something of an embarrassment to Addison when he came to publish it, for the Queen did him the honour to hint that she would accept the dedication. Yet for Addison to have dedicated the play to the Queen would have implied, in view of her recent quarrel with the Marlboroughs, that he accepted the Tory interpretation of the play as hostile to the Duke.[2] The hint was tactfully ignored and the play published without a dedication; its political ambiguity was thus not dispelled.

For Drury Lane the result of the great success of *Cato*, beyond the substantial profits, was the entry of Barton Booth into the

---

[1] *Apology*, ii. 26–27.

[2] Peter Smithers (*The Life of Joseph Addison* [Oxford, 1954], pp. 256–7) writes: 'Addison had intended to dedicate the piece when published to an unidentified person, probably Sarah, Duchess of Marlborough. He was embarrassed by those who made *Cato* a Tory play and such a dedication would have made his loyalty quite clear. The queen, however, intimated that she would be pleased if asked to accept a dedication herself, a high but embarrassing honour.' Mr. Smithers's interpretation of Addison's motives seems to me incompatible with the information conveyed by Pope to Spence.

management and the consequent retirement of Thomas Doggett. Even before the run of *Cato* Booth had clamoured for admission to full partnership with Cibber, Wilks, and Doggett; and because he enjoyed the support of powerful courtiers (according to Theophilus Cibber he was an intimate of Bolingbroke),[1] his claim could not be ignored. Cibber cites, as a reason for the managers' reluctance to accept him as a partner, Booth's failure to co-operate with the actor-managers several years earlier in their struggle for independence from Christopher Rich. As early as 16 December 1712, four months before his triumph in *Cato*, Booth wrote to Lord Lansdowne, appealing to him as to a friend of higher rank, to recommend his cause (presumably admission to the management) to the Vice-Chamberlain.[2] During the month after the production of *Cato*, Cibber and Booth were active rivals at Court. They 'used frequently to set out', Theophilus Cibber wrote, 'after Play (in the Month of *May*) to *Windsor*, where the *Court* then was, to push their different Interests'.[3] To make it more difficult for Booth to get to Windsor, the managers scheduled plays in which he had a principal part every night; but with the aid of a nobleman who lent him a chariot and six he managed to get to Windsor nevertheless and yet return to the theatre in time for the performance the following night.[4] Booth gained his end. A new theatrical licence was issued, on 11 November 1713, in which Booth's name was included along with the names of Collier, Cibber, Wilks, and Doggett.[5] Soon thereafter Doggett retired, in part as a protest against the Court's forcing the managers to accept Booth.

Openly neither Whig nor Tory, Drury Lane flourished during Anne's last years, enjoying a monopoly of the legitimate drama in London. With the exception of *Cato*—which, with Addison's precautions, was safe enough—the actor-managers avoided plays that might prove dangerous in the inflammatory political atmosphere. Propaganda plays were written and sometimes published. One of them, *The General Cashiered* (1712),

[1] *The Life and Character of . . . Barton Booth, Esq.* (London, 1753), p. 6.
[2] B.M., Add. MS. 38607, p. 9.
[3] Theophilus Cibber, *Life of Booth*, p. 7.
[4] W. R. Chetwood, *A General History of the Stage* (London, 1749), pp. 92–93.
[5] P.R.O., L.C. 5/155, p. 261. (Cited in Nicoll, *Early Eighteenth Century Drama*, p. 276.)

is a curious allegory of Marlborough's dismissal. But they did not attain production at Drury Lane in those years of Boling-broke's vigilance. Journalistic criticism of Drury Lane, not yet sharpened by party animus, was in the main genial and appro-batory; the theatre basked in the favour of Steele's praises in *The Tatler*, *The Spectator*, and *The Guardian*. The baiting of Cibber, in later years a major avocation of journalists, had not yet begun. All this changed suddenly with the accession of the new King.

IV

THE THEATRES IN PARTY RIVALRIES,
1714–28

THE decisive Whig victory which coincided with the accession of George I established for all to see the direction that political power would follow, and the actor-managers of Drury Lane were prompt to associate themselves with the winning side. At the same time they apparently tried to associate their rival theatre, Lincoln's Inn Fields (which opened under John and Christopher Mosier Rich late in 1714) with the discredited Tories. There seems to have resulted, in a limited sense, a Drury Lane claque and a Lincoln's Inn Fields claque: the former Whig, Hanoverian, and after the mid-1720's pro-Walpole; the latter Tory (either Hanoverian or Jacobite) and, in the later years of the reign, anti-Walpole. There was nothing firm about all this, but the patterns of political allegiance in the theatres, like the patterns of political allegiance in friendships, were usually discernible and occasionally emphatic.

As we have seen, two of the three actor-managers then active, Booth and Cibber, seem to have had political ties with the Tories before the Queen died; but in the new reign Drury Lane became forthrightly Hanoverian and Whig. First of all, the actor-managers exchanged their Tory partner, William Collier, for a distinguished Whig, Richard Steele, an exchange made possible by the automatic termination of the company's theatrical licence upon the death of Queen Anne.[1] Moved in part by gratitude to Steele for the dramatic notices in *The Tatler* and *The Spectator*, Cibber, Wilks, and Booth invited him (rather than Collier) to join them in petitioning for a new licence; and when he did so the petition was promptly granted, in October 1714.

Three months later, in January 1715, the theatrical licence was replaced by a patent, a more secure legal instrument,

---

[1] Loftis, *Steele at Drury Lane*, Part I.

conveyed by the King to Steele alone but assigned in part by him to the actor-managers. This patent was similar in the powers it authorized to the patents Charles II had granted to Killigrew and D'Avenant, though unlike the earlier ones this was limited in its duration—to Steele's lifetime and three years thereafter. Steele and his colleagues interpreted it as freeing them from dependence on the Lord Chamberlain and his subordinates. After the patent passed the Great Seal, they ceased submitting plays for licensing to the Master of the Revels; and in several minor episodes of theatrical routine they refused submission to him and even to the Lord Chamberlain.[1]

John Rich and Christopher Mosier Rich (about whom little is heard) jointly inherited their father's share, by then apparently a dominant one, in the theatrical patent deriving ultimately from the grants to Killigrew and D'Avenant.[2] The elder Rich, it will be recalled, was silenced by the Lord Chamberlain in 1709; but although forbidden to exercise his patent rights during Anne's lifetime, he retained them, and upon the accession of George received permission to open Lincoln's Inn Fields, which he had hopefully rebuilt while under the order of silence. He died before he could open the theatre, but his sons carried on.[3] Thus the pattern of theatrical competition was established that persisted throughout the reign of George I: Steele and the actor-managers at Drury Lane, John and Christopher Mosier Rich at Lincoln's Inn Fields—the one theatre noisily Whig, the other under the suspicion of Tory and even Jacobite sympathy.

The managers of Drury Lane made the most of their identification with the Whigs—or so it appears from frequent demonstrations at the theatre. Some of these demonstrations, such as a special prologue spoken by Wilks in honour of the King just after his arrival in London in 1714,[4] can be discounted as the conventional and politic tributes to a new monarch, but the vivacity of party spirit in the theatre exceeds the conventional. Newspapers alone provide substantial documentation of Drury

[1] Loftis, *Steele at Drury Lane*, pp. 121 ff.
[2] Nicoll, *Restoration Drama*, pp. 331 ff.
[3] Cibber, *Apology*, Chs. XII, XIII, XV; Avery, *London Stage*, I, xxxii-xxxiv.
[4] The prologue was probably written by Steele: Rae Blanchard (ed.), *The Occasional Verse of Richard Steele* (Oxford, 1952), pp. 68-69, 106-7.

Lane's fervour: *The Original Weekly Journal*, 17–23 March 1716, and *The Weekly Journal; Or, British Gazetteer*, 24 November 1716 and 5 January 1717, printed prologues and epilogues containing Whig declarations; whereas *The Flying Post*, 26 February–1 March 1715, introduced a doggerel poem about the Tories with an allusion to their hissing the last new play presented there (presumably Charles Johnson's *The Country Lasses*, the epilogue of which glances satirically at the Tories' 'separate Peace').[1] As already noted, in *The Freeholder*, No. 34 (16 April 1716), Addison mentioned the excess of zeal at Drury Lane.

In the face of Drury Lane's pugnacious insistence on its own loyalty, Lincoln's Inn Fields was forced to the defensive. As early as 1715 a dramatist complained of the injustice done the theatre by the popular belief that it was Tory in sympathy:

> But here we cannot forbear Reflecting on One more particular Hardship upon the *Muses*, that is, the too popular Outcry, that the *Theatres* are *Party-Houses*; the *Governours*, or *Masters* of the *New Play-House* [Lincoln's Inn Fields], being maliciously represented to be of a contrary Inclination to those of the *Old* One. How this villainous Suggestion took Rise is unaccountable, when 'tis well known, there cannot be warmer Zealots, or more hearty Devotees to the present Government, than the *Founders* and *Proprietors* in that House; more especially the two Young Gentlemen, the nearest concern'd in it, it being a Principle suck'd in with their very Milk.[2]

Again, an epilogue spoken at the theatre on 5 April 1716 carries this burden:

> Whatev'r t'other House may say to Wrong us,
> We have, as well as they, some honest WHIGS among us.[3]

More frequently, the defensive note is sounded in protests against the usurpation of the stage by party.[4] Christopher

---

[1] Commenting on a performance of *The Spanish Friar* at Drury Lane, 9 November 1715, the diarist Dudley Ryder wrote (ed. William Matthews, London, 1939, p. 181): 'I observed that most of the clappings were upon party accounts. There happened to be some reflections upon the priests which the Whigs clapped extremely and the Tories made a faint hiss.' (Quoted from Avery, *London Stage*, i. 389.)

[2] Preface to anonymous, *Wit at a Pinch; Or, The Lucky Prodigal* (London, 1715).

[3] Printed in *The Weekly Journal; Or, British Gazetteer*, 7 April 1716.

[4] Cf. prologues to Charles Molloy, *The Perplexed Couple* (1715); to Charles Knipe, *The City Ramble* (1715); and to John Leigh, *Kensington Gardens* (1720).

Bullock, a leading member of the Lincoln's Inn Fields company,[1] protested at length in his *Woman Is a Riddle* (December 1716) against the introduction of politics into the drama:

> But now you [critics] judge from Passion, not from Reason;
> All Wit's thought Factious, and all Satyr—Treason

he complains in the prologue. And in the first act of this gay comedy of intrigue (which otherwise is virtually a translation of Calderón's *La Dama Duende*), there occurs an exchange that sounds like an authentic report:

Courtwell: If you are not dispos'd for Drinking, will you go to the Playhouse, there's a new Comedy to be acted to Night?

Colonel Manly: I nauseate the Place; 'tis become worse of late than a Coffee-House: The Rage of Party is so Predominant, that ev'n publick Diversion is interrupted, and 'tis impossible to sit out a Play with any Satisfaction, for the ridiculous Comments which a Man is oblig'd to hear from the Politicians in the Pit.

Courtwell: That is a publick Grievance indeed, and not to be redress'd, but by a general Consent of the Persons who frequent the Theatres, by resolving to go only for their Diversion, without the poor Satisfaction of indulging their Spleen.

Colonel Manly: In short, the old Plays are so curtail'd for fear of giving Offence to Parties, that if *Shakespear*, *Fletcher*, and *Johnson* were alive, they'd hardly believe their Productions legitimate; and for New Plays, there can be none worth seeing, since the Viciousness of the Age has beat out Satyr's *tripple* row of Teeth by a kind of general Consent.

(Ironically, this play, in which Bullock writes so indignantly against the rage of parties, is dedicated to Philip, Marquis and later Duke of Wharton, who in the autumn just preceding the first performance of the play had visited the Pretender at Avignon and had drunk his health in Paris at the table of the English ambassador.)[2]

The decade of the 1720's heard the same complaints at Lincoln's Inn Fields. The prologue to Eliza Haywood's *The Fair Captive* (March 1721) alludes to the damaging effect of party feuds on state and stage, and John Sturmy's *The Compromise* (December 1722) takes the destructiveness of party

---

[1] In at least the season of 1717–18, he participated in the management of the theatre: Avery, *London Stage*, II. 461.

[2] *DNB*, s.v. Wharton. Cf. Alexander Pope's satirical portrait of him in his epistle *To Sir Richard Temple, Lord Viscount Cobham*, ll. 174–209.

feeling as its theme. The play, not unlike Benjamin Griffin's *Whig and Tory*, produced at the same theatre two years earlier, uses the political antagonism of two old gentlemen who are parents or guardians of young lovers, as the obstacle to be overcome before the lovers can be united.[1] In the prologue of William Phillips's *Hibernia Freed* (February 1722), there is a satirical hit at those who 'in Party, strong,/Through five dull Acts their Politicks prolong'. As in the previous decade, protestations against party feeling came from the theatre under some suspicion of disaffection, not from the noisily 'loyal' Drury Lane.

The seriousness of Drury Lane's suspicions of Lincoln's Inn Fields is indicated in a letter that Steele wrote the Lord Chamberlain in September 1721, in which he protested the theatre's use of the title 'Theatre Royal' in its play notices. This title, so Steele maintained, properly applied only to Drury Lane:

> For either from some fancy that by Printing Theatre Royall they hope to evade the punishment may fall upon deserters [actors who had left Drury Lane to join Lincoln's Inn Fields], or that they intend a reall insult on the Kings Authority (which they have notoriously and frequently done in Licentious Allusions in their prologues, Epilogues and other incidents) or whatever is their motive they have, in their Bills presumed to write *Theatre Royall*.
>
> I will not trouble Your Grace with many Arguments why more especially in this case than any other the Word Royall should be appropriated to the King on the Throne, but shall only, at present, Leave it to Yr Grace's consideration, how many matters which seem light may be drawn into greater moment and Consequence from any the Least Ambiguity on publick occasions, when You reflect that the Crowd Assemble themselves, even in their Pleasures, according to their inclinations in Politicall Affairs.
>
> I hope Your Grace will not imagine I speake wholly from my interest in this case, if I repeat to you that it will be matter of Scandal to the Sober part of our Audience, who are most Zealous

---

[1] Mrs. Centlivre's *The Artifice*, produced at Drury Lane in October 1722, provides an informative contrast with Sturmy's *The Compromise*. In both plays political antagonism complicates the love intrigue of a young couple, but in Mrs. Centlivre's there is no observance or recommendation of impartiality between political extremes. The complication is the disinheritance of the young man by his Jacobite father for loyally breaking up a meeting of non-jurors. There is, in brief, an emphatic Whig and Hanoverian note in Mrs. Centlivre's play in contrast with a studied neutrality in Sturmy's.

for His Majesties' Service, if those who remarkably Urge Particular Circumstances in Plays, to the Disadvantage of the Government, should be Protected, or Shelter'd in that Practise By the Use of the Kings Own Name.[1]

Steele's charges apparently had some grounds. Political discontent, not to mention downright rebelliousness, could scarcely appear openly. But newspaper notices suggest that members of the company were less cautious than the dramatists. *The Weekly Journal; Or, British Gazetteer*, 10 June 1721, printed an announcement suggesting at once disaffection at Lincoln's Inn Fields and the theatre's responsibility for some of the numerous journalistic attacks on Drury Lane: 'Mr. Griffin of the New Play-House, has been under Examination before the Committee for Seditious Libels, on account of Mr. Mist's Paper.' Again, *The St. James's Journal*, 29 November 1722, included a notice that 'On Monday Mr. Ogden, one of the Actors at the Theatre in Lincoln's Inn Fields, was committed to Newgate for treasonable Words'. And *The Daily Journal*, 21 January 1723: 'On Saturday last Mr. John Ogden, late a Comedian of the New Play-House, was try'd before the Bench of Justices at Hick's-Hall for cursing his Majesty, &c.' The reports of the different means taken in 1724 by Pinkethman of Drury Lane and Marshall of Lincoln's Inn Fields to celebrate the anniversary of the King's accession provide a striking contrast. Pinkethman in Richmond displayed a flag, lighted bonfires, and provided music and liquor for the crowd that assembled;[2] Marshall rode through London in a turnip cart, wearing a crown and a pair of horns on his head and a mask on his face—until he was arrested in Great Russell Street and committed to prison.[3]

The devotion to the House of Hanover displayed by Drury Lane was in a measure repaid by royal favour. The company enjoyed conspicuously more command performances than Lincoln's Inn Fields; and in the autumn of 1718 it presented a series of plays at Hampton Court (thus reviving the old custom of Court performances), for which the managers were handsomely paid.[4] The King himself, who knew little English,

---

[1] Blanchard (ed.), *Correspondence of Steele*, p. 166.
[2] *The Daily Post*, 3 August 1724.
[3] *The British Journal*, 8 August 1724.
[4] There is a warrant, dated 15 November 1718, to pay Steele for the company the sum of £574. 1s. 8d. (Aitken, *Steele*, ii. 189–90.)

seldom went to the theatre, but the Prince of Wales went often, and his patronage helped Drury Lane in its competitive struggle with Lincoln's Inn Fields.[1]

In an effort, apparently, to help Lincoln's Inn Fields in its turn, a group that included Lord Brooke raised a subscription for the theatre in about 1718. We know little about the episode —not enough to say positively that it had political implications. The prologue of Elkanah Settle's *The Lady's Triumph* (March 1718), 'Spoken to the Subscribers', expresses the theatre's gratitude for deliverance from a tyrannical power and from a 'prejudice' which may well have been political. Early in 1720 John Leigh, an actor in the Lincoln's Inn Fields company, dedicated his *Kensington Gardens* (produced at the theatre in November 1719) to Lord Brooke, to whom Leigh expresses gratitude for 'the noble Example you have shewn, in being the first Subscriber towards the Support of our Theatre'. One of the few facts known about William, Baron Brooke (1694– 1727), beyond the bare sequence of the important dates in his life, is that he was a Tory.[2]

The most controversial of the political plays at Drury Lane during these years were Charles Johnson's *The Cobbler of Preston* (1716) and Colley Cibber's *The Non-Juror* (1717), both of which touched off skirmishes with Lincoln's Inn Fields, described humorously and no doubt with a modicum of truth by George Akerby in a pamphlet entitled *Spiller's Jests* (1729). Akerby relates that James Spiller, an actor of Lincoln's Inn Fields, obtained a copy of the principal role of Johnson's play several weeks before the play was ready for the stage by picking Pinkethman's pocket during a drinking bout; and that Christopher Bullock, working from suggestions thus obtained, prepared a rival farce also called *The Cobbler of Preston*, which was produced at Lincoln's Inn Fields before Johnson's reached the stage at Drury Lane.

Now I would have the *Reader* to observe [Akerby continues], that Mr. *Bullock*, who always prided himself upon his Attachment to the Principles of *Toryism*, not only robb'd the above-mentioned ingenious Mr. *Charles Johnson* of great Part of the large Profits which he

[1] Cibber, *Apology*, ii. 169.
[2] George Edward Cokayne, *The Complete Peerage*, s.v. Brooke.

expected from the Run of a *Farce*, which was wrote, so much to the
Support, and the Defence of the *H - - - - - r Succession*, but wrote his
own Farce, call'd *The Cobler of Preston*, likewise in quite another
Manner, turning into Burlesque and Ridicule all Mr. *Johnson's*
Thoughts and Designs, and giving Spirit to the Party which Mr.
Johnson had rendered contemptible and Spiritless. . . .

To strengthen our Suspicion of Mr. *Spiller's* unhappy Sentiments,
with regard to the G- - - - - - - -t, and to shew the mutual Confidence
that seemed to subsist between Mr. *Christopher Bullock* and him,
I shall now take Notice of another Farce, call'd *The* PERJUROR,
wrote likewise by the abovesaid Mr. *Christopher Bullock*, which was
acted in Opposition to the NONJUROR, a Comedy written by
that undoubted *Lover* of, and *Ornament* to his Country, Mr. COLLY
CIBBER, and in which Mr. *Spiller* bore a considerable Part, and spoke
a Prologue to it, which gave Mr. *Cibber* and the *Court-Party* no small
Chagrin.[1]

The tone of this account assures us that it is far from literal
truth; yet, apart from the detail of Spiller's picking Pinkethman's pocket, there is little in what Akerby says that is not
supported by the objective facts. A clumsy farce by Christopher
Bullock called *The Cobbler of Preston*, obviously put together
hastily, was produced at Lincoln's Inn Fields on 24 January
1716; a longer play of the same title written by Charles Johnson,
a much better farce that surely took more time to write, was
produced at Drury Lane on 3 February 1716. Both farces are
adaptations of the Christopher Sly episode in *The Taming of the
Shrew*, and both make capital of the current interest in Preston
Heath, where the Jacobite rebels had just been captured.
Johnson's is a Whig farce, a satirical rendering of the follies of
the Preston Jacobites. It is an overstatement to say that Bullock's
turns into 'Burlesque and Ridicule' Johnson's Hanoverian
principles, for Bullock's farce, apart from its setting and some
veiled jokes at the expense of Nonconformist ministers, has
nothing to do with the Rebellion or the discontent that inspired it. Bullock's motive seems to have been mercenary
rather than political, and his play, anticipating Johnson's,
perhaps hurt attendance at Drury Lane.

So also with his *The Perjuror* the following year. The title

---

[1] [George Akerby], *Spiller's Jests: or, The Life and Pleasant Adventures of the late
Celebrated Comedian Mr. James Spiller* (London [1729]), pp. 24–25.

was clearly meant to suggest Cibber's *Non-Juror*, as Bullock acknowledged in his prologue:

> All you that come, expecting Party-Wit,
> As sure as you're alive now, you are all bit.
> No doubt your Expectations all were big,
> That this Per-juror was a furious Whig . . . .

Yet the play itself, about the machinations of a corrupt country justice of the peace, has nothing to do with Cibber's play and little to do with the political situation that provided its background.[1] To be sure, the farce satirically condemns the sin of perjury, and it implies that those who take oaths freely, without scruple of conscience (the audience would have thought of the oaths to the new King) may be more reprehensible than those who are prevented by conscience from taking them. Cibber was no doubt recognized in the person of Spoilem, the leader of a group of strolling players brought before the Justice of the Peace. In answer to the Justice's question 'What Religion are you of?' Spoilem answers:

> Religion!—Hum!—Why truly I have not fix'd upon any yet, nor I believe shan't, till the Times are settled.

There are several such satirical glances at the crude chauvinism of Cibber's play; but open criticism of Cibber's theme was in the nature of things impossible.

---

[1] The trick of presenting plays with politically suggestive titles was used more than once by Lincoln's Inn Fields, whose dramatists might deplore the intrusion of party into drama but were none the less aware of their audiences' preferences. Earlier, in May 1716 the company had presented a tragedy with the name *Cato of Utica*, which three years after the first performance of Addison's famous play would have aroused the expectation of political innuendo. The prologue alludes to the first *Cato*, asserting that this play too has liberty as its theme; and the epilogue strikes at those who would accept masters from France or Rome. However, the tragedy itself, a translation by John Ozell from the French of Deschamps, appears innocent of political intention and certainly attracted no political enthusiasm from the indifferent audiences who saw it.

Still another play with a title chosen to arouse the expectation of party clamour that the author had no intention of satisfying is Benjamin Griffin's *Whig and Tory* (1720), and this time the trick is frankly acknowledged in the prologue. The party champions who provide the excuse for the title are only the politically minded fathers of two couples of young lovers, whose stratagems to achieve matrimony (in no important way different from those of scores of contemporary dramatic characters) supply the major interest. The political struggle, to be sure, is a constant frame of reference; the love intrigue is conducted against a background of talk about politics, the burden of which is that party strife is regrettable. But it is all scarcely more than timely jest.

Drury Lane's vigorous effort in support of the Hanoverians reached a climax with *The Non-Juror*. Produced in December 1717, when the excitement over the rebellion of two years earlier was subsiding, the play excoriated the Jacobites with a jingoistic fury. All the subtlety of Molière's *Tartuffe*, from which it is adapted,[1] is lost in this blatant exercise in demagoguery, produced after the cause it purported to defend was already won. Yet the play was an immense success.[2] It ran sixteen nights in December and was afterwards revived. Cibber received permission to dedicate it to the King, an honour that was accompanied by a gift of £200. Thereafter until his death Cibber's voice was among the loudest in the chorus of praise of the Hanoverians, whose Poet Laureate he became in 1730. As he himself observed, the subject of the play was its protection. No one could take issue with its theme, though critics could and did maintain that he violated propriety by using religious zeal as a subject for dramatic satire.[3] The play made enemies for Cibber, both of persons whose principles he opposed, and of others who, though loyal Hanoverians, objected to the play's crudity and demagoguery. A battery of anonymous pamphlets, most of them hostile, appeared in its wake,[4] and Cibber began to figure regularly as a subject of ridicule in the pages of disaffected newspapers. It is from this time that Cibber dates his unpopularity.[5] Two years before, however, in *Town Talk*, No. 2, Steele had included an anecdote of Cibber's unpopularity, jocosely attributed by Steele to his appearance on the stage in the roles of villains.

Steele and the actor-managers, as I have suggested, all but declared their independence from the Lord Chamberlain and his subordinates when early in 1715 they received a theatrical

---

[1] In making his adaptation Cibber employed an English translation of *Tartuffe* by Matthew Medbourne: Dudley H. Miles, 'The Original of *The Non-Juror*', *PMLA*, xxiii (1915), 195–214. *The Non-Juror* has a strong resemblance to Crowne's *The English Friar* (1690), which satirizes Catholic influence in the time of James II; but *Tartuffe*, in Medbourne's translation, was Cibber's principal source.

[2] Dudley H. Miles, 'The Political Satire of *The Non-Juror*', *Modern Philology*, xiii (1915–16), 281–304; 'A Forgotten Hit: *The Non-Juror*', *Studies in Philology*, xvi (1919), 67–77.

[3] Mist's *Weekly Journal*, 28 December 1717; *The Entertainer*, 25 December 1717.

[4] See Nicoll, *Early Eighteenth Century Drama*, p. 190 n.

[5] *Apology*, ii. 186–7.

patent. During the tenures as Chamberlain of the Duke of Shrewsbury (1714–15) and the Duke of Bolton (1715–17), no reprisals were taken against them, though records of legal queries suggest that Bolton contemplated action.[1] When in April 1717 the Duke of Newcastle succeeded to the office, he insisted more vigorously on his prerogatives; and he soon came into conflict with Steele and the managers. The ensuing dispute was thus fundamentally a jurisdictional one, turning on the overlapping authorities of Lord Chamberlain and patentee; but in its development it became entangled with national politics to such an extent that the political issues eventually overshadowed the jurisdictional ones. The Parliamentary debates of 1719 and 1720 found Steele and Newcastle on opposite sides in the Whig schism, Steele following Robert Walpole in opposition to the Ministry led by Stanhope and Sunderland, which Newcastle supported. Although Cibber was not active in politics, he made known his agreement with Steele on the disputed issues.[2] It was at least in part as an act of political retaliation that the Duke moved first against Cibber and afterwards against Steele, silencing the actor for several weeks and suspending Steele for a period which in the event proved to be nearly a year and a half. Only after Robert Walpole came to power following the South Sea disaster was Steele restored to his post at Drury Lane.[3]

The action against Steele had brought a chorus of approval from the large number of persons who desired closer governmental supervision of the theatres. From the time of the Collier controversy there had been demands for stricter controls, and the demands had continued, though the grounds on which they were based shifted somewhat. Many of the complaints about Drury Lane turned on the actor-managers' reluctance to accept new plays for production, because, so the critics charged, they could fill their house with old ones without the expense of authors' benefit nights. To these critics, the Lord Chamberlain's intervention seemed the hopeful inauguration of a new era in which aspiring authors could be heard.[4]

---

[1] Loftis, *Steele at Drury Lane*, pp. 122–3.

[2] By his praise of Steele's political independence in the dedication to him of the tragedy *Ximena* (September 1719).

[3] Loftis, *Steele at Drury Lane*, pp. 127–58.

[4] Ibid., Part III.

It was John Dennis who described most comprehensively the issues of theatrical government implicit in the action against Drury Lane. Even before the controversy reached a crisis, Dennis in 1719, moved by personal pique, addressed several sharp letters to Steele and to Booth. Describing 'the Degeneracy of the Publick Taste', Dennis concluded gloomily that 'as the general Taste of *England* could be never said to be good, it was never so bad as it is at present'.[1] The managers, he charged, exploited the public taste and made no attempt to improve it. After both he himself and the Lord Chamberlain had been further provoked by the managers, Dennis in November 1719 addressed the dedicatory epistle of *The Invader of His Country* to Newcastle, urging him to assert the authority of his office over Drury Lane: 'It being evident from Fact, that all our principal Dramatick Poets and Players have been form'd while our Theatres were under the Lord Chamberlain's Regulation; and that both Writing and Acting have gradually fall'n off, since the Players have pretended to exclude him from his Jurisdiction over them'.[2] Actors, Dennis believed, were by training, by personal interest, and even by profession, inadequate arbiters of the national drama; and in a prose satire of 1720, directed against Steele and the actor-managers, he explained in detail why he thought so.[3]

Steele was committed to a contrary position, and he was led by his dispute with Newcastle to an extended exposition of it in a biweekly periodical, *The Theatre* (January to April 1720),[4] and a pamphlet, *The State of the Case between the Lord Chamberlain of His Majesty's Household and the Governor of the Royal Company of Comedians* (March 1720). Under the terms of the theatrical patent, Steele insisted at length, he and the actor-managers, to whom he had assigned joint rights, were solely responsible for Drury Lane; and in support of his contention that their independence was not only legal but desirable, he praised the profession of the actor, as elsewhere he had often done before. Since he had left the conduct of routine affairs to the actor-managers, he was compelled to maintain, against such detrac-

---

[1] 'To Judas Iscariot, Esq; On the Degeneracy of the Publick Taste', in *Critical Works*, ed. Hooker, ii. 171.
[2] Ibid. 179.
[3] *The Characters and Conduct of Sir John Edgar*, in ibid. 181–217.
[4] Ed., John Loftis (Oxford, 1962).

tors as Dennis, their capacity for managing a theatre. And he found it prudent to maintain also that Drury Lane, as well as English drama generally, was in a flourishing condition. In the flurry of pamphleteering with which his writings were greeted, his position received some support; but the opposition, for which Dennis was the most articulate spokesman, had the better of the debate.[1]

Steele's suspension from his post at Drury Lane was terminated in May 1721, not upon settlement of the disputed principles of theatre government, but upon the change in his political fortunes that came with Walpole's rise to first place in the Government. The questions raised concerning the respective authorities of patentee and Lord Chamberlain were not answered, if indeed they were answerable without legislation. As in the years before Steele received his patent, the Lord Chamberlain and his subordinates continued to intervene occasionally, but there seems not to have been a return to a systematic censorship by the Master of the Revels.[2] The actor-managers for the most part went their own way, after 1724 without Steele, who was compelled by debts and bad health to retire to Wales.

Complaints about the actor-managers, and about their competitor John Rich at Lincoln's Inn Fields, continued; and with them continued the demands for closer governmental supervision of the theatres. As the decade of the 1720's wore on, critics came to be more and more incensed at the 'non-rational' entertainments—the entertainments, that is, of singing, dancing, juggling, and especially pantomime that supplemented the play of the evening. The critics were all but unanimous in the opinion that the distinction between traditional comedy and tragedy, on the one hand, and the supplementary entertainments, on the other, represented the distinction between an appeal to the rational faculties and to the non-rational or

---

[1] Among those who supported Dennis's contention that the Lord Chamberlain should, for the health of dramatic literature, maintain a close supervision of the theatres were the anonymous authors of *The State of the Case . . . Restated*, of *The Anti-Theatre*, and of *The Crisis of Honesty*. At least one of the participants in the debate, however, the author of an essay which appeared in Applebee's *Original Weekly Journal*, 28 May 1720, acknowledged in informative detail the practical difficulties inherent in close supervision of the theatres by the Lord Chamberlain.

[2] Cf. White, 'The Office of Revels', loc. cit., pp. 23–25.

merely sensual.[1] Whether or not the managers of the theatres agreed with the critics, they felt themselves forced by the realities of theatrical finance to continue to present the entertainments. 'If I am ask'd (after my condemning these Fooleries myself)', wrote Cibber in his *Apology*, 'how I came to assent or continue my Share of Expence to them? I have no better Excuse for my Error than confessing it. I did it against my Conscience! and had not Virtue enough to starve by opposing a Multitude that would have been too hard for me.'[2] From the terms of Cibber's defence—and essentially the same argument was used by Steele as early as 1715[3]—it is easy to see why many critics felt that the direction of the theatres should not be entrusted to persons who were motivated by a desire for profit. 'If the Managers of the Playhouses should have either the Obstinacy or Covetousness to persevere in sacrificing all the Glory of the Theatre to their own mercenary Views', wrote a critic in *The Weekly Journal; Or, British Gazetteer*, 10 September 1726, 'I heartily wish, it may not be thought unworthy the Consideration of the Civil Power, to interpose its Authority against so poisonous and arbitrary a Proceeding.' Dennis's arguments are but the most explicit of many that governmental supervision was needed to prevent the managers from prostituting the theatres to the degraded taste of audiences.

The widespread dissatisfaction with Drury Lane under the actor-managers and Lincoln's Inn Fields under John Rich gave rise to proposals for the establishment of a national academy of drama. Englishmen trying to discover a way out of the dramatic doldrums would have been aware of the successes of the French national theatre across the channel; and they would have been aware, too, of the recently established Royal Academy of Music, devoted to the performance of operas.[4] To this latter the actor-

---

[1] Emmett L. Avery, 'The Defense and Criticism of Pantomimic Entertainment in the Early Eighteenth Century', *ELH, A Journal of English Literary History*, v (1938), 127-45.
The theoretical objections expressed to the supplementary entertainments resemble those to the newly imported Italian opera, though in the case of opera theoretical criticism was reinforced by English nationalistic resentment of a foreign art form and by the circumstances of theatrical competition. (See Siegmund A. E. Betz, 'The Operatic Criticism of the *Tatler* and *Spectator*', *Musical Quarterly*, xxxi [1945], 318-30.)   [2] *Apology*, ii. 181-2.   [3] In *Town Talk*, No. 2.
[4] For an account of the Royal Academy of Music, see Avery, *London Stage*, i. lxxi-lxxx.

managers refer in a letter of December 1724 addressed to their partner, Steele:

> There are several persons of Fortune, that, we have reason to believe, wou'd be glad to purchase our Interests [in the Drury Lane patent], and put it upon the Foot of the Opera by fixing the Direction into an *Academy*, which is, we think, the only Way to support & perpetuate the English Theatre.[1]

The despondency expressed here was proved by the subsequent history of Drury Lane to be unwarranted; the theatre soon recovered from the depression into which it had fallen, and the managers gave over thoughts of withdrawing from it. Their remark, however, in a letter written without thought of publication, suggests the drift of opinion among men with experience in trying to meet public taste.

Although by this time in retirement because of his health, Steele had earlier attempted, over a period of ten years, to establish a theatrical organization to which he referred as an 'academy'.[2] He conceived the scheme about 1712, apparently influenced in doing so by the Renaissance academies;[3] and he continued his efforts in support of it until about 1722, though it was not successful in any measure approaching his expectations. In his most sanguine plans, he envisaged a society of 200 ladies and gentlemen who would subscribe to a varied series of semi-dramatic entertainments, prominent among which would be recitations of poetry against a background of music. He called the project by a name with an appropriate double meaning, the 'Censorium'. He shared the interest of the Renaissance academicians in the interrelated effects of music and poetry on the human passions, having been led to the subject, I suspect, by the huge success of Italian opera in combining poetry and music. He hoped to see an organized, perhaps incorporated, group conduct the Censorium; and for a while he tried to interest Oxford, then Lord Treasurer, in it. Governmental support or support by subscription, had it been forthcoming,

---

[1] Blanchard, ed., *Correspondence of Steele*, pp. 184–5. A critic writing earlier in the same year in the journal *Pasquin* (21 January 1724) also used the Royal Academy of Music as an example of a desirable form of theatrical organization.

[2] Loftis, *Steele at Drury Lane*, pp. 98–118.

[3] On the Renaissance academies, see Frances A. Yates, *The French Academies of the Sixteenth Century* (The Warburg Institute, University of London, 1947).

would have enabled the Censorium to exist without the necessity to meet the public taste—a debilitating necessity in the
opinion of Steele as of later projectors of academies.

A detailed and extended organizational plan for a national
academy of drama was published in 1732.[1] It bears resemblance
to a burlesque 'Project for the Advancement of the Stage',
which appeared as the final chapter of Pope's pre-*Dunciad*
commentary on the literary scene, *Peri Bathous* (1728). Pope's
'project', ostensibly a summary of an earlier proposal made
by Dennis and Gildon,[2] is a grandiose scheme for the formation of a dramatic academy. His satirical intent precludes our
accepting the details of the scheme as representing a particular
serious proposal; but had there not been talk about the formation of an academy—and about its organization—we may be
sure Pope would not have included the chapter.[3]

All the talk about a national academy of drama came to
nothing, although some of the desired ends to be gained by one
—restriction of theatrical competition, closer governmental
supervision—were gained, albeit in perverted form, by the
Licensing Act of 1737. It is important to note that the special
attractions of a dramatic academy were the prospects of
closer governmental supervision and of escape from the profit
motive. Most theatrical commentators wanted less not greater
freedom in the theatres; and far from thinking that competition
between theatres was a stimulus to the production of good
drama, they saw in it a degrading and vulgarizing force. The
popular taste was low, they believed, and if the theatres were
driven by competition to try to please it, the drama would
suffer. Steele expressed a common attitude in his *Town Talk*
when he attributed the shortcomings of Drury Lane to the

---

[1] In pamphlet form as *A Proposal for the Better Regulation of the Stage*, it was largely
reprinted in *The Weekly Register*, 5 February 1732.

[2] Dennis and Gildon's *A New Project for the Regulation of the Stage* was advertised
in the *Daily Post*, 5 February 1720, as just published. Despite diligent search by
modern scholars, however, no copy of the pamphlet has been discovered—if indeed it ever existed, for Pope conceivably could have arranged for publication of
the advertisement as preparation for his burlesque. (Cf. James Sutherland, ed.,
The Dunciad [The Twickenham Edition of the Poems of Alexander Pope, 2nd
ed., 1953], p. 197.)

[3] In 1719 Gildon published a plan for a comprehensive literary (not specifically dramatic) academy. (G. L. Anderson, 'Charles Gildon's Total Academy',
Journal of the History of Ideas, xvi [1955], 247-51.)

managers' need to compete with Lincoln's Inn Fields;[1] and Cibber in his *Apology* when he described the existence of more than one theatre as a demoralizing influence on drama.[2] Walpole was at least moving in the direction recommended by most critics when he reduced the number of theatres and placed them under closer supervision by the Lord Chamberlain.[3]

In these years when Jacobitism was a present danger, the occasion of rebellion in 1715 as again thirty years later, hatred and fear of Catholicism was a corollary of devotion to the constitutional principles established in 1688. Tragedies dramatized incidents that illustrated the alleged iniquity of the Catholic Church, which was depicted as a corrupt institution propagating an unscrupulous political absolutism and denying liberty of conscience. As portrayed by the dramatists—by Nicholas Rowe, Ambrose Philips, George Sewell, and Charles Beckingham, among others—the Catholic Church represents the antithesis of English constitutional monarchy. The latter was conceived to be established on law (constitutional principle based in turn on natural law); the former on superstition, the very perversion of natural law. For the most part dramatists, out of a sense of decorum, kept their hostility to the Catholics out of comedy (Cibber in *The Non-Juror* excepted); but they felt no compunction about introducing it into tragedy, regarding the dignity of the genre as justification for the religious theme.

Nicholas Rowe's *Lady Jane Grey*, produced at Drury Lane amid the vehement declarations of loyalty to the Protestant Succession in 1715 and thus in the year when the dramatist became Poet Laureate, is as thoroughly a propaganda piece as his early *Tamerlane*. Rowe this time celebrates Protestant firmness in opposition to Catholic tyranny as he had earlier English liberty in opposition to French absolutism. His choice as heroine of one who died at the hands of Catholics in defence of the Reformation was determined by his desire to animate opposition to Jacobitism in that year of rebellion. But his

[1] No. 2.
[2] Ch. XV.
[3] The title of Watson Nicholson's *The Struggle for a Free Stage in London* (Boston and New York, 1906) is, I believe, misleading in so far as it applies to the early eighteenth century. The 'struggle' was rather for closer governmental regulation

success as propagandist was at the price of failure as tragic dramatist. *Lady Jane Grey* shares the weaknesses characteristic of his tragedies, but they are exaggerated: the heroine is more passive than usual, the threatening force more malevolent and unyielding, the course of dramatic action more starkly simple, the pathos of the catastrophe more emphatically elaborated in non-functional metaphor. Only the inflamed passions engendered by the fear of Jacobitism could have led Rowe to the crude propaganda of the final scenes. 'Death or the Mass attend you' (v), says the Bishop of Winchester to Lord Guilford, Lady Jane's husband. And he nobly replies:

> 'Tis determin'd;
> Lead to the Scaffold.

Tragedies founded on anti-Catholic themes were not the property of Drury Lane alone. In 1719 the management of Lincoln's Inn Fields produced two that were scarcely less vehement in their hostility than *Lady Jane Grey*: Charles Beckingham's *King Henry IV of France* and George Sewell's *Sir Walter Ralegh*. Neither is a good play, though the former is the more patently frigid and declamatory. Like Dryden and Lee in *The Duke of Guise*, though with a different purpose, Beckingham found in the French religious wars of the sixteenth century a parallel to the later English dynastic and religious controversies.[1] In his dedicatory epistle he refers to the similarity between events in the life of Henry IV and recent events in England. 'Will not the World be before-hand with me in the Application, and bring the Parallel down very near to our own Times?' he writes, presumably referring to the rebellion of 1715. He depicts an abortive rebellion, whose leaders vainly hoped to gain strength from a discontented religious minority—not Catholics in this instance but Huguenots. However, the play's chief target is Catholic bigotry and intolerance: a Papal nuncio and a bishop in the first act recall with satisfaction the recent massacre of 200,000 Protestants by members of the Holy League. 'Such ever be the Doom', exclaims the bishop,

---

[1] On the subject of the historical parallels, see Salmon, *The French Religious Wars in English Political Thought.*

and such the Fate
Of that impassive, that repugnant Tribe
Of unconforming Hereticks.

Although a Huguenot turned Roman Catholic, Henry IV is an enlightened monarch whose conception of the kingly office resembles that of post-Lockeian Whigs; he explains the futility of religious persecution, of 'War upon Mens Minds' (1) so convincingly as to suggest that Beckingham was writing with a knowledge of Locke's *Letter Concerning Toleration*. A Catholic monarch thus speaks for the principles of political and religious freedom which in England in 1719 were associated with the Protestant Succession.

Sewell's tragedy dramatizes the closing episode of Sir Walter Ralegh's life—the events preceding his execution by James I on the insistence of the Spanish ambassador, Gondomar—and thus allows its author to excoriate English Court intrigue with Catholic powers. Because Ralegh as admiral, adventurer, explorer, and founder of colonies had been an obstacle to Spanish ambition, the tragedy could also emphasize England's continuing rivalry with Spain, which in the course of 1718 reached briefly the intensity of open warfare. The utterances of Ralegh resound with the theme of England's imperial destiny,[1] which two decades later was to become a dramatic commonplace. The customary anti-Jacobite note is thus complicated by the added dimension of imperial ambition.

The pervasive influence on drama of the fear of Jacobite rebellion may be seen in the adaptations from Shakespeare. 'The whole cluster of adaptations of Shakespearean tragedies from 1720 to 1723,' concludes a recent study of the subject, 'indeed point the single moral. Each one deals with faction and uprising: Dennis's *Invader of His Country*, Theophilus Cibber's *Henry VI*, Lewis Theobald's *Richard II*, Buckingham's *Julius Caesar* and *Marcus Brutus*, Hill's *Henry V*, and Ambrose Philips' *Humfrey Duke of Gloucester*.'[2] Dennis explained at length his patriotic motive in undertaking the adaptation of *Coriolanus* which he called *The Invader of His Country*; and we may assume that the other dramatists who, at about the same time, altered

---

[1] Cf. Act IV.

[2] George C. Branam, *Eighteenth-Century Adaptations of Shakespearean Tragedy* (Berkeley and Los Angeles, 1956), pp. 62-3.

G

Shakespeare had similar reasons for doing so. In a winter, he writes (in a complaint about the actor-managers' postponement of the play), when England was threatened with double invasion, from Sweden on the north and Spain on the west, its production would have been 'most seasonable'.[1] If overemphatic in his insistence on England's danger, Dennis conveys a sense of the times that produced political plays in such profusion. Coriolanus, the invader of the title, represents the Old Pretender, who like the Roman joined 'with foreign Foes,/T'invade or to betray . . . [his] Native Country [v]'. Whatever the ambiguity of Shakespeare's political moral, Dennis's theme is clear enough, at the sacrifice, however (as is the rule in propaganda plays), of subtlety in characterization.[2]

The temper of tragedy in George I's reign is aptly suggested by a journalistic critic who in 1731 glanced back over the dramatic consequences of Addison's *Cato* (which he praises):

But *Cato* itself has increased the Evils of the present Time, how many Poetasters have since then infested the World with wild Notions of Liberty and Patriotism! What strange romantick Whims have they had of Freedom, and Independency from Power! As if, as Mr. *Dryden* says,

They led their wild Desires to Rocks and Caves,
And thought that all, but Savages, were Slaves.[3]

Plays with settings all over the world and in all epochs of history resound with praise for the conception of constitutional monarchy that emerged from the Revolution. Dramatists seem to have searched for historical figures or episodes that could provide examples either of contemptible tyranny or of noble defiance of tyranny. Ancient Egypt in Edward Young's *Busiris* (1719), ancient Ireland in William Phillips's *Hibernia Freed* (1722), ancient England in Ambrose Philips's *The Briton* (1722), and ancient Spain in Philip Frowde's *The Fall of Saguntum* (1727) all become locales for the declamation of Whig principles. The steady iteration of the apostrophes to liberty and freedom in times and places that are fictionally remote ulti-

---

[1] Dedication to *The Invader of His Country*. In *Critical Works*, ed. Hooker, ii. 177.
[2] Cf. Branam, *Adaptations of Shakespearean Tragedy*, pp. 125-7.
[3] *The Universal Spectator, and Weekly Journal*, 10 April 1731. Reprinted in John Loftis (ed.), *Essays on the Theatre from Eighteenth-Century Periodicals* (Augustan Reprint Society, 1960), pp. 15-19.

mately establishes the illusion that Whig political philosophy is founded on immutable natural law. The dramatists could after all control the political forces operating in their tragedies; and they made them operate in the manner described by Locke in *The Second Treatise of Government*.

As I have already said, the tragedies with 'loyal' themes (whether original plays or adaptations from Shakespeare) appeared at both Drury Lane and Lincoln's Inn Fields. Dramatic themes are, after all, easily discerned by audience and critic, altogether too easily for the disaffected group at Lincoln's Inn Fields (assuming, as seems likely, that such there was) to have made itself heard in drama except perhaps in innuendo. To be sure, Drury Lane produced the most distinctly Whiggish comedies, Cibber's *The Refusal* (1721) and Steele's *The Conscious Lovers* (1722), but it also produced comedies that dramatized the social philosophy long associated with the Tories. No doubt the greater volume of Whig propaganda in both comedy and tragedy was heard at Drury Lane, but this may have been due not so much to calculated managerial policy as to the theatre's association with a prominent group of Whig dramatists, who now felt none of the restraints they had known under Queen Anne.

The degree to which the stage was usurped by politics in these years may be read in the dramatic criticism of the journals. The prosperous beginnings of periodical criticism of the drama in Steele's essays did not meet conditions favourable to development; rather than enjoying an independent life, dramatic criticism became in the journalistic warfare of the second and third decades of the century a tool of political controversy. 'If we except the remarks on plays and players by the authors of the Tatler and Spectator,' Thomas Davies wrote late in the century, 'the theatrical observations, in those days, were coarse and illiberal, when compared to what we read in our present daily and other periodical papers.'[1] And a chief reason for the coarseness and illiberality was the preoccupation with politics; that political bias coloured much of the early eighteenth-century journalistic commentary on the theatre is a self-evident fact to anyone familiar with the files,

[1] Thomas Davies, *Dramatic Miscellanies* (London, 1783-4), iii. 480.

say, of Mist's *Weekly Journal*, Applebee's *Weekly Journal*, *The Grub Street Journal*, or *The Craftsman*. Yet the preoccupation with politics, though pervasive, was in no sense complete; then as at any other time the motives that led to dramatic criticism were complex and individual. Even the newspaper party organs did not sacrifice all sense of dramatic values to their overlords, who usually had more important matters on their minds.

As already noted, Drury Lane under the actor-managers was linked with the Hanoverians against the Jacobites and later with the Walpole against the anti-Walpole Whigs, and Lincoln's Inn Fields was to some degree identified with the opposing groups. We would therefore expect the Jacobite papers to be more friendly to Lincoln's Inn Fields and the Walpole papers to Drury Lane. And as a general rule they were.

Mist's *Weekly Journal* provides the most obvious instance of political bias determining theatrical commentary. Cibber's attribution of its animus to resentment of *The Non-Juror* is an oversimplification, but only that. The start of Mist's sustained attacks on Drury Lane coincides with the production of *The Non-Juror*; and, as Cibber wrote, 'for about fifteen Years following, [*The Weekly Journal*] scarce ever fail'd of passing some of his Party Compliments upon me: The State and the Stage were his frequent Parallels, and the Minister and *Minheer Keiber* the Menager were as constantly droll'd upon'.[1] With surprising pertinacity the newspaper, high Tory in bias,[2] kept up an abusive commentary on Drury Lane affairs, in which Lincoln's Inn Fields often figured as the theatre deserving encouragement.

The bond between Lincoln's Inn Fields and Mist's journal may have been a close one. Benjamin Griffin of that theatre (as noted above)[3] was examined in 1721 by the Committee for Seditious Libels because of an association with *The Weekly Journal*, and Charles Molloy, who had three plays produced

---

[1] *Apology*, ii. 187.

[2] On the subject of the political affiliations of the journals, see D. H. Stevens, *Party Politics and English Journalism, 1702–1742* (Chicago, 1916); Laurence Hanson, *Government and the Press, 1695–1763* (London, 1936); and William T. Laprade, *Public Opinion and Politics in Eighteenth Century England* (New York, 1936). In 1723 a printer, Samuel Negus, prepared an informative if biased memorandum in which he classified journals according to their political complexions (printed in John Nichols, *Literary Anecdotes of the Eighteenth Century* [London, 1812–15], i. 289ff.).

[3] See above, p. 68.

at the theatre, wrote for the paper.[1] The amount of space that the paper gave to criticism of Drury Lane affairs, much more space than any other journal gave to a theatre, can be most plausibly explained, as Cibber explained it, in political terms. The Tory writers for Mist's, of whom John Gay became one, found in the alleged corruption of the Drury Lane management a useful symbol for the alleged corruption of Walpole's Government.[2] Only rarely did the journal print anything that could properly be called dramatic criticism; the many references to Drury Lane, to Lincoln's Inn Fields, and to the plays they produced can more accurately be described as party-inspired gossip.[3]

Dislike of the Hanoverians and, after his Ministry was established, of Walpole again coincides with vehement dislike of Drury Lane in Applebee's *Original Weekly Journal*, a moderate Tory journal drawn to theatrical comment by the activities of Richard Steele, the Whig—and Walpole Whig—governor of Drury Lane. Applebee's, which during most of its run ignored the theatre, displayed a tenacious and unfriendly interest in Drury Lane's affairs in 1720 owing to the dispute between Steele and the Duke of Newcastle. From February to July 1720, with periods of intermission, the journal devoted space liberally to attacks on Steele and his colleagues in the management. Taken in isolation Applebee's hostility to Drury Lane could scarcely be attributed to political animus, but when viewed in the context of political and theatrical biases, it falls neatly into place. The dominant interest of the paper was political and, except for this series of attacks on Drury Lane, it gave little attention to the theatres.

Because most of the journals were vehicles for party propaganda, they refrained from comment on the theatres except when such comment could serve a political end—as when Drury Lane produced Cibber's *The Non-Juror*. Journalistic response to it followed party lines. We have seen that the Tory Mist's *Weekly Journal* was the play's most vociferous critic. Conversely, its most outspoken defender was the Whig paper,

[1] Laprade, *Public Opinion and Politics in Eighteenth Century England*, p. 248.
[2] Cf. D. H. Stevens, 'Some Immediate Effects of *The Beggar's Opera*', in *Manly Anniversary Studies in Language and Literature* (Chicago, 1923), pp. 180-9.
[3] For a comprehensive analysis of dramatic criticism in the journals, see Charles Harold Gray, *Theatrical Criticism in London to 1795* (New York, 1931).

Read's *Weekly Journal*. Read printed a puff, with political coloration, on 7 December 1717, the day after the play's first performance: 'Last Night the Comedy call'd the Nonjuror, was Acted at his Majesty's Theatre in Drury-Lane, which very naturally displaying the villany of that most wicked and abominable Crew, it gave great Satisfaction to all the Spectators.' The following week Read included a laudatory notice of the play, containing a synopsis of the action, and on 4 January 1718 printed 'The Prologue, written by N. Rowe, Esq; to the incomparable Comedy, call'd, The Nonjuror and spoken by Mr. Wilks', as well as 'The Epilogue spoken by Mrs. Oldfield'. The first of Mist's counterblasts appeared 28 December 1717, in the form of a letter from a correspondent objecting to Cibber's use of a matter of conscience. 'Let any one who knows any thing of the Institution and Rules of the Drama, consider this Piece', the correspondent continues, 'and then say, whether the Author does not equally offend against Art and good Sense, Religion and good Manners.' In the same letter he significantly praises 'another Play, lately acted at the New House, called the Perjurer, by way of Opposition to the Nonjuror'. Just three days earlier, on 25 December 1717, a 'high flying' periodical called *The Entertainer* had criticized Cibber's subject with even more force, repeating the objection expressed earlier by Jeremy Collier, Daniel Defoe, and a number of others to the institution of the stage itself. Mist included, on 1 March 1718, a further letter containing criticism of the play, as well as abuse of Cibber; the letter was signed 'Charles Johnson' and dated from Button's Coffee House (ironically, it would seem, since Johnson was a Drury Lane Whig and Button's a meeting-place for Drury Lane wits). Beyond the comment it evoked from the journals, *The Non-Juror* occasioned a spate of politico-critical pamphlets.

Unlike *The Non-Juror*, Steele's *The Conscious Lovers* is political only in the sense that it dramatizes Whig social philosophy, and yet it, too, evoked journalistic comment that followed party lines. It was greeted by the town as a theatrical event of importance, a publicity campaign of unprecedented proportions having prepared the way for it;[1] and the newspapers allotted considerable space to critical examinations of it. With-

---

[1] Loftis, *Steele at Drury Lane*, pp. 194-5.

out exception, the papers that were sympathetic to the play were well disposed toward the Hanoverians, whereas those unfriendly to it were not. *The St. James's Journal*, it is true, though a loyal organ of the Walpole ministry, printed several critical essays on the play in which strictures appear; but the tone of these essays, in which *The Conscious Lovers* is respectfully considered as a major literary event, is distinctly favourable. The hostile papers were Mist's and *The Freeholder's Journal*, both of them conspicuous 'high flyers'. To Mist's the play merely provided an occasion for further gibes at the group in charge of Drury Lane. *The Freeholder's Journal* (which otherwise showed little interest in the theatre) printed an extended series of derogatory though well-reasoned critical essays. These essays contain no political comment; the stated objections to the play are literary; and yet the fact of the sustained hostility to it and indeed to Steele himself in a political journal of a Tory cast that usually ignored the stage could scarcely have been without political meaning. The anonymous critic on 12 December 1722, in commenting upon Steele's dedication to the King, significantly associated it with Cibber's five years earlier: 'Was it not enough, that so Wise, so Amiable a King, punish'd himself in Countenancing the *Nonjuror*, but that the *Conscious Lovers* must also rush into his Presence?'

The journal's strictures on the play did not go unanswered, in pamphlets as well as newspapers. Of the three newspapers that printed laudatory notices, two of them by way of answering the criticisms of *The Freeholder's Journal*, all were loyal Hanoverians—*The Whitehall Journal*, *The Whitehall Evening Post*, and *The Postman*. Yet if politics provided a motive for this controversy, its issues as debated by the journalistic critics were literary.

Although the actor-managers of Drury Lane seem to have been 'loyal' to Walpole from the time he became chief Minister, papers sympathetic to him did not always support Drury Lane. In fact, papers of all political persuasions were united in condemning the policy common to the management of both Drury Lane and Lincoln's Inn Fields of presenting 'non-rational' entertainments. For example, the journal *Pasquin*, founded by Walpole late in 1722,[1] printed a series of discussions

---

[1] Stevens, *Party Politics and English Journalism*, p. 115. The journal was possibly

of the theatres, in which were repeated the customary laments
that the managers of the theatres—Drury Lane as well as its
competitors—were debasing the stage with spectacle and
music: 'the Dancing-Master and the Joyner usurp both the
Profits and the Applause which are due only to the Writer and
the Actor [4 February 1724].' Writing as one concerned only
with the artistic problems of drama, the author of these essays
revealed no partiality to any of the theatres. So also with
discussions of the stage that appeared in the pro-Walpole
Read's *Weekly Journal* during 1726. Here both major theatres
are criticized, and the burden of the complaint is again the
mercenary subordination of artistic accomplishment to sound
and spectacle. Just as Drury Lane came under criticism from
journals sympathetic to Walpole, so also did Lincoln's Inn
Fields from those hostile to him—from Mrs. Eliza Haywood's
The Tea Table (1724), for example, in which frequent criticism
of both theatres coincides with veiled criticism of the Ministry.
There were only a few politically disinterested journals in this
period, but there were some, including Aaron Hill's *The Plain
Dealer*, which expressed disapproval of the managerial practices
of both theatres.[1]

As the decade of the 1720's advanced and as the association
of Drury Lane with Walpole became more firm after *The
Beggar's Opera*, it probably became more difficult for journalists
to ignore political considerations when writing about the
drama. But the political coloration was important all along.
Certainly if we depended exclusively on the journalistic comment for information, we should gain a distorted view of the
theatres. We should gain, for example, little awareness of the
substantial artistic accomplishment of Drury Lane, which
year after year ably produced many plays of high literary
quality.

In May 1721, only a month after Walpole became First
Lord of the Treasury and Chancellor of the Exchequer, he
took a hand in Drury Lane affairs, restoring Steele to his

written by Duckett: George Sherburn, *The Early Career of Alexander Pope, 1688–1727*
(Oxford, 1934), p. 225.
    [1] For an account of the journal, see Dorothy Brewster, *Aaron Hill: Poet, Drama-
tist, Projector* (New York, 1913), pp. 156 ff.

position as governor. Steele's suspension, as I have said, had been in part an act of political retaliation for his support of Walpole against the Stanhope Ministry in the Whig schism of the years just before the South Sea Bubble. 'This Violation of Property', Steele wrote on 9 April 1721, referring to the action against his theatrical patent, 'I take to have been instigated by the late Secretaryes Stanhope and Craggs for my opposition to the *Peerage* Bill by Speeches in the House and Printed Pamphlets'.[1] There may have been political grounds for an alliance between Walpole and Drury Lane, although we must remember that the stage could have occupied only an infinitesimal portion of his ministerial attention in the years before *The Beggar's Opera*. Yet Steele, who remained in the House of Commons, would have served as a link between the theatre and the Government until he retired to Wales in 1724.

Drury Lane produced no propagandistic plays favourable to Walpole, and indeed none seem to have been written; but it avoided satirical attacks on him. The only instance that I have found of a satirical hit at him during the years of the actor-managers occurs in a pantomimic entertainment presented in November 1724, John Thurmond's *Harlequin Sheppard; A Night Scene in Grotesque Characters*. In the published version, which probably represents only an approximation of what appeared on the stage, John Gay's *Blueskin Ballad*[2] is printed after an account of Blueskin's cutting Jonathan Wild's throat—presumably indicating that the ballad was sung. And the ballad makes the equation of statesman, inevitably understood as Walpole, with thief (later to become so famous in *The Beggar's Opera* and *Jonathan Wild*):[3]

> Some cheat in the Customs, some rob the Excise,
> But he who robs both is esteemed most Wise.

The date of *Harlequin Sheppard* is early, when the opposition was just forming, and when the cry of corruption was just beginning to be sounded. Probably it was because the lines

---

[1] Blanchard (ed.), *Correspondence of Steele*, p. 541.
[2] On the ballad, see William Henry Irving, *John Gay, Favorite of the Wits* (Durham, N.C., 1940), pp. 204–6.
[3] On this equation, see William R. Irwin, *The Making of Jonathan Wild* (New York, 1941), pp. 22–31.

of faction had not yet been firmly drawn that the pantomime with its pointed innuendo was permitted at Drury Lane.

It was not until about 1725 that the literary opposition to Walpole, in time to become so raucous, was organized.[1] Earlier the political associations of the two playhouses mainly reveal the older Whig and Tory stamp.[2] The literary society at Button's Coffee House, a stronghold of the Whig wits since its founding under Addison, seems to have been influential at Drury Lane well into the 1720's—which is scarcely surprising since both Cibber and Steele were prominent there. Ambrose Philips, long one of the Buttonians, had plays produced at Drury Lane in 1722 and in 1723: *The Briton* and *Humphrey, Duke of Gloucester*. An anonymous writer in the Tory Applebee's *Original Weekly Journal*, 12 March 1720, in introducing a series of essays on abuses in literature, asserted with indignation that he would 'examine what Right *Button's Coffee-House* has to the decision of Wit and good Sense, tho' Sir *John Edgar* [Steele] or *Cyberini* be Chairmen'. And another writer, similarly anonymous, concluded a criticism of *The Conscious Lovers* in *The St. James's Journal*, 15 December 1722 (in which Pope's Atticus lines appeared for the first time in print), with a complaint: 'that the Reputation of my Understanding ought to rise or fall at *Button's* Coffee-House, just as my Subject happens to lead me to censure or commend the Transactions of the Neighboring Stage, is certainly very unjust Usage of your Humble Servant.'[3]

During these early years of the decade the literary criticism of Walpole was confined to the attacks, bitter but lacking the pungency of high talent, of a group of journals. And as I have already suggested several of these journals (Mist's, Applebee's, *The Freeholder's*) were severely critical of Drury

---

[1] Charles Bechdolt Realey, *The Early Opposition to Sir Robert Walpole* (Philadelphia, 1931), pp. 158–9. Cf. J. H. Plumb, *Sir Robert Walpole: the King's Minister* (Cambridge, Mass., 1961), pp. 141–3.

[2] The political entanglements of the two theatres about 1723 are suggested in a curious pamphlet by Gabriel Rennel, *Tragi-Comical Reflections, of a Moral and Political Tendency, Occasioned by the Present State of the Two Rival Theatres in Drury Lane and Lincoln's Inn Fields*. Rennel develops a prolonged parallel between the activities of the two theatres and the two political parties, associating Drury Lane with the Whigs and Lincoln's Inn Fields with the Tories.

[3] Button's partiality for Drury Lane over Lincoln's Inn Fields was noted in *The Freeholder's Journal*, 12 December 1722.

Lane. We may see in them a transition from hostility to the theatre grounded in Jacobitism to a hostility grounded in hatred of Walpole.

Those Tory wits who were above the level of Grub Street demonstrated a progressive antagonism to Drury Lane, quite marked after the appearance of *The Beggar's Opera*. Their reasons, I suspect, were less political than personal—dislike of Cibber, whose prominence in the management made the theatre a natural object of attack in the war against the dunces which was fairly under way years before Pope's poem first appeared in 1728. Pope and Gay quarrelled with Cibber as early as 1717 over Drury Lane's treatment of *Three Hours after Marriage*,[1] and hostilities between the wits and the actor continued intermittently. Drury Lane presented Gay's *The Captives* with moderate success in 1724, though the event seems not to have brought about cordial relations between him and the managers. In the first version of *The Dunciad* Pope handled Cibber freely, if not so conspicuously as in the final version; but he satirized Cibber's competitor John Rich as well. We think of his later boast in *An Epistle to Dr. Arbuthnot*: 'The Play'rs and I are, luckily, no friends.' The political dimension in the animosities was at most latent.

The relations of Pope's chief dunce, Lewis Theobald, with the two theatres provide a suggestive instance of a parallel between literary and political alignments.[2] For several years before 1728 Theobald served Rich as a writer of prologues and pantomimes, and in 1726 he dedicated to him his *Shakespeare Restored*. Until 1727 he seems to have been on unfriendly terms with the actor-managers of Drury Lane.[3] But in December of that year Drury Lane produced his pseudo-Shakespearian discovery *The Double Falsehood*, and when it was published soon after, Theobald wrote warmly of the actor-managers, attempting, it would seem, to make amends for his earlier hostility. So

---

[1] George Sherburn, 'The Fortunes and Misfortunes of *Three Hours After Marriage*', *Modern Philology*, xxiv (1926–7), 105–7. On Pope's relations with Cibber, see Malcolm Goldstein, *Pope and the Augustan Stage* (Stanford, 1958).

[2] On Theobald's career, see Richard Foster Jones, *Lewis Theobald* (New York, 1919).

[3] In the preface to his adaptation of *Richard II* (performed at Lincoln's Inn Fields, December 1719), he had criticized them at a time when they were under duress from the Lord Chamberlain.

far as we can judge, he took little interest in politics, although, to be sure, Pope in *The Dunciad Variorum* of 1729 accused him of writing for Mist's *Weekly Journal*.[1] The implication in Pope's charge that he was Tory troubled Theobald, probably because at that time he hoped for favours from the Ministry. In 1730 he was recommended for the Poet Laureateship by both Walpole and the Prince of Wales,[2] circumstances indicating that he was politically acceptable. Thus Theobald, after some eight years of alienation from the actor-managers during which time he was under suspicion of writing for a Tory paper, patched up his quarrel with Drury Lane in the same season (1727-8) that Lincoln's Inn Fields produced *The Beggar's Opera*, bitterly anti-Walpole, and Pope published *The Dunciad*, severely censorious of Theobald as well as of the managers of both theatres. And two years later Theobald, with some backing from Walpole, was a leading contestant for the Laureateship. It would appear significant that Theobald, after some mild association with the Tories, should turn his hopes to the Walpole Whigs and make up with Drury Lane just when John Rich alienated Walpole by producing *The Beggar's Opera* and Pope attacked Theobald and all the managers in *The Dunciad*. However, there was no break between Theobald and John Rich; Theobald's pantomimes continued to appear at Lincoln's Inn Fields.

Political differences there were between Lincoln's Inn Fields and Drury Lane in the early and mid-1720's. But their rivalry did not follow consistently the distinction between Court party and opposition. Plays produced at Lincoln's Inn Fields as well as at Drury Lane were, in published form, dedicated to Walpole or a member of his family.[3] The theatrical rivalry of these years was more concerned with the efforts of the two companies to outdo each other in pantomime than with anything else. But with the appearance of *The Beggar's Opera*, politics became a far more important issue in the theatres.

The condition of the stage and the drama was unsatisfactory

---

[1] Book I, l. 192 (Sherburn, *Early Career of Pope*, p. 241).

[2] Jones, *Theobald*, p. 147.

[3] Robert Hurst dedicated *The Roman Maid* (Lincoln's Inn Fields, 1724) to the Lady Walpole, daughter-in-law of the Minister; James Moore Smythe dedicated *The Rival Modes* (Drury Lane, 1727) to Walpole himself; and Philip Frowde dedicated *The Fall of Saguntum* (Lincoln's Inn Fields, 1727) to him.

in George I's reign, and everyone who did not have a vested interest in the theatres was ready to say so. The vehemence and the bulk of the journalistic rebuttal of Steele's defence of Drury Lane in *The Theatre* and the extensive discussion of the formation of an academy of drama provide a measure of public resentment of the managers and of despair for the future so long as the theatres responded to the profit motive. Yet officials in the Government showed little inclination to consider problems of theatre supervision apart from issues of national politics. Steele was suspended when he went into opposition to the Stanhope–Sunderland Ministry; he was reinstated when Walpole, whom he had supported, gained first place. So long as George I reigned, Walpole found nothing in the theatres to displease him; and the Lord Chamberlains, who followed his lead, were content to let the managers go their own way. So indifferent was the Government to the theatres that such regulatory machinery as existed was allowed to fall into disrepair. The time of reckoning was coming in the new reign.

V

THE THEATRES IN OPPOSITION,
1728–37

IF the accession of George II in 1727 did not inaugurate a new
era in the theatres, the production of Gay's *Beggar's Opera* in
1728 certainly did. The temper of the theatres in the following decade grew far more belligerent than it had been since the
Restoration. For lack of evidence we cannot say whether Cibber
refused *The Beggar's Opera* on political grounds when it was
offered to Drury Lane; but refuse it he did, to the good fortune
of John Rich. The astonishing success of *The Beggar's Opera* at
Lincoln's Inn Fields capped the opposition's propagandistic
triumphs in *Gulliver's Travels* and *The Craftsman* and gave new
courage to the opponents of Walpole, who for the first time saw
fully how effective the stage could be as a medium for propaganda.[1] Whereas political allusion earlier had been cautious
and mostly loyal to Sovereign and Ministry, after 1728 it
became bold and often hostile, occasionally (by innuendo) to the
King himself and much more often to the King's first Minister.
The mass of abuse directed at Walpole during these years
resembles nothing so much as the bursting forth of a drunken
man's long-repressed bad temper. Walpole took no decisive
action, however, until Fielding improved on Gay's example;
finding the older pattern of governmental supervision inadequate
to control the hostility, he finally resorted to the stern repressive
measure of the Licensing Act of 1737.

The Beggar's Opera is curiously genial to have had important
political consequences. Not an allegorical play nor even one with
characters consistently identifiable with living figures, it scores
its hits by way of a succession of political parallels, each established briefly and then obscured as different character relationships emerge. Thus Macheath the robber of the public gives
way as a symbol of Walpole to Peachum the screen, the receiver

---

[1] Stevens, 'Some Immediate Effects of *The Beggar's Opera*,' loc. cit.

of stolen goods, who with his brother-in-law plies a profitable trade in legitimate peculation. All this is reinforced by deft allusion to vices that had long been charged to Walpole—graft, bribery, treachery, and adultery. Accompanying the political commentary and preventing it from becoming insistent were the gay songs, rich in every kind of innuendo, and the accumulated wealth of traditional melodies.[1]

The opposition press cheerfully elucidated the opera's political meaning. When a play like *The Conscious Lovers* could become entangled in party conflict, it is small wonder that the most delightful and most telling dramatic satire of the eighteenth century should have divided critics along political rather than literary lines. The compelling nature of the opera's satire put objective criticism quite out of the question. For supporters of Walpole, a wounded silence or a counterattack were the only alternatives; for the vociferous opposition, the opera provided an opportunity to be gleefully seized. Even 'Caleb D'Anvers' of *The Craftsman*, whose preoccupation with politics seldom left room for dramatic criticism, gave liberal space to praises of it. Gay himself, as well as Swift and possibly Pope, was a contributor to *The Craftsman*, and none of them would have been likely to miss so fair an opportunity for satirical hits at the common enemy (it is impossible, however, to identify their separate contributions).[2] The journal provided extended commentaries under a light cloak of irony on the political meaning of the play—as, for example, in a letter to D'Anvers from 'Phil Harmonicus' printed in the number of 17 February 1728. 'There are some Persons who esteem *Lockit*, the Keeper, or *prime Minister* of *Newgate*, to be the *Hero* of the Piece,' writes Phil Harmonicus, in allusion to Walpole and Townshend, 'to justify which Opinion, they take Notice that He is set forth, on the Stage, in the Person of Mr. Hall, as a very *corpulent bulky* man, and that He hath a *Brother* named *Peachum*, who, as represented by Mr. *Hippisley* appears to be a *little, awkward, slovenly* Fellow.' Phil Harmonicus believes, on the contrary, that Captain Macheath is the principal character and that it is he who was drawn 'to asperse *somebody in Authority*'. The opera thus becomes a starting-point

---

[1] For a comprehensive account of the play, see William E. Schultz, *Gay's Beggar's Opera* (New Haven, 1923).

[2] Stevens, 'Some Immediate Effects of *The Beggar's Opera*,' p. 185.

for further jokes at Walpole's expense; it is not the subject of dramatic criticism.

Swift contributed to *The Craftsman*, as I have said, and he may have written one or more of the notices on *The Beggar's Opera*; it is impossible to be sure. But he is known to have contributed an essay on the opera to a Dublin periodical, *The Intelligencer* (No. 3),[1] not long before 6 July 1728, when the essay was reprinted in Mist's *Weekly Journal*. Swift here wrote with his eye fixed more firmly on Walpole than on *The Beggar's Opera*; he resented Walpole's allegedly ungenerous treatment of Gay, a treatment inspired, according to him, by Gay having been falsely suspected of writing a lampoon on Walpole. Although Walpole was convinced that Gay did not write the lampoon, Swift observed with a glance at the gossip about Lady Walpole's infidelity, 'having lain under the Suspicion, it seemed very just, that he should suffer the punishment; because in this most reformed Age, the Virtues of a Prime Minister are no more to be suspected, than the Chastity of *Caesar*'s Wife'. Swift's irony serves faction as well as dramatic criticism; hence Nathaniel Mist's interest in the essay.

Mist had joined in the journalistic sport with *The Beggar's Opera* several months before he reprinted Swift's essay, but apparently not before 2 March 1728, four and a half weeks after the play first appeared at Lincoln's Inn Fields. A curious delay, in view of Mist's customary attention to theatrical events with political overtones, perhaps to be explained by fear of governmental reprisals, for in these years Mist was frequently subjected to legal action.[2] The journal's opening sally was a doggerel poem that revealed hostility in jibes at actors and actresses of Drury Lane. Mist apparently gathered courage as time passed, since on 23 March he printed an attack on Walpole that takes its starting point from Gay's song:

> When you censure the Age,
> Be cautious and sage,
> Lest the Courtiers offended should be.

The song no doubt struck a responsive chord in the breast of Nathaniel Mist; the special grievance animating his attack of 23 March seems to be the prosecution of opposition writers.

---

[1] In Herbert Davis (ed.), *Prose Writings of Jonathan Swift*, xii. 32–37.
[2] Cf. Laprade, *Public Opinion and Politics*, pp. 278, 307.

Walpole's hostility notwithstanding, Mist continued from time to time to divert the town with party sallies stemming from the opera—as on 29 June, when he reported a 'Rumour that *Polly Peachum* is gone to attend the Congress at Soissons, where, it is thought, she will make as good a *Figure*, and do her Country as much Service, as several others that shall be nameless'.

Mist's implied charge that Walpole was prosecuting opposition writers was justified. For if Walpole was not moved to strict repressive measures by the intensified criticism of the Government, journalistic and dramatic, that followed upon the opera's success, he was none the less forced to take some defensive actions. He prosecuted *The Craftsman* and Mist's *Weekly Journal* during 1728 and 1729, and at the same time increased his subsidies to existing government journals and backed a new one, *The Senator*, a major purpose of which was to oppose the political satire in *The Beggar's Opera*. He seems to have backed John Mottley's farce *The Craftsman* (Little Theatre in the Haymarket, October 1728), the title of which indicates the butt of its satire; and he forbade the production at Lincoln's Inn Fields in 1729 of Gay's *Polly*, the sequel to *The Beggar's Opera*.[1]

Polly is no more a systematic political allegory than its predecessor, but it carries on the implied equation of courtiers and felons, even though the felons in this instance have been transported to America. The dimmest wit in a London audience would have caught the innuendo in the title character's explanation of what had happened to her father (i): 'My Papa kept company with Gentlemen, and ambition is catching. He was in too much haste to be rich. I wish all Great Men would take warning. 'Tis now seven months since my Papa was hang'd.' It is perhaps less remarkable that Walpole refused to tolerate *Polly* than that he should have put up with *The Beggar's Opera*. We learn of the method of suppression from the preface to the published play: 'After Mr. *Rich* and I were agreed upon terms and conditions for bringing this Piece on the Stage,' Gay writes, 'and that every Thing was ready for a Rehearsal; The Lord Chamberlain sent an order from the country to prohibit Mr. *Rich* to suffer any Play to be rehears'd upon his Stage till it had been first of all supervis'd by his Grace [the Duke of Grafton].' Walpole, on whose suggestion the King issued the appropriate

---

[1] Cf. Stevens, 'Some Immediate Effects of *The Beggar's Opera*,' loc. cit.

order to the Lord Chamberlain,[1] must already have known the nature of the play—as in the London of that era how could he have failed to.

When *Polly* was suppressed, the opposition turned in resentment on Drury Lane—and on Cibber, who as so often before provided a ready target. Early in 1729, just as the town learned of the order to John Rich, Cibber produced a ballad opera of his own, *Love in a Riddle*. It was rumoured, Cibber writes in his *Apology*,[2] that he himself secured the suppression of *Polly* in the interest of his own play, a rumour which, he plausibly says, was as flattering in its suggestion of political capability as it was malicious and false. *Love in a Riddle* was a weak play, the success of which under any conditions would have been doubtful; in the face of the uproar aroused by the irate supporters of Gay, it had no chance at all. Yet Cibber's losses in the Ministry's behalf were amply compensated in the following year when, upon the death of Laurence Eusden, he was made Poet Laureate—not so much for his service to literature, as he and everyone else recognized, as for his friendship with influential noblemen[3] and for his political service.

The growing audacity of dramatic satire in this period marked the weakening of the Government's control of the stage. A further indication of weakening if not indeed breakdown in the regulatory machinery was the increase in the number of theatrical companies. From the stable theatrical situation of George I's reign, with Drury Lane and Lincoln's Inn Fields the only theatres consistently offering legitimate drama, the situation became in George II's early years more complex and competitive.

Since 1720 there had been in addition to the 'opera house' a second theatre in the Haymarket, the so-called 'Little Theatre', built by a carpenter named John Potter apparently as a speculative venture.[4] Until about 1728 the theatre housed chiefly

[1] John, Lord Hervey, *Some Materials Towards Memoirs of the Reign of King George II*, ed. Romney Sedgwick (London, 1931), i. 98.

[2] *Apology*, i. 246–8.

[3] Barker (*Cibber*, pp. 156–8) attributes the appointment to Cibber's friendship with the Duke of Grafton.

[4] For an account of the theatre, see Avery, *London Stage*, i. xxxv–xxxvi; ii. 591; illustration facing i. 158.

transient and foreign companies;[1] and, although it operated without a theatrical patent, it seems to have aroused little opposition until the early years of George II, when its greater activity and increased prosperity brought it into legal trouble. The theatre gained prominence from 1728 to 1730, when plays by Samuel Johnson of Cheshire and Henry Fielding were presented, and much more prominence from 1735 to 1737, when Fielding led the company performing there. Meanwhile, another theatre without benefit of formal patent had entered the competition for audiences, this one in Goodman's Fields and thus in East London. Opened in 1729 by Thomas Odell, who apparently had some kind of royal authorization, transferred in 1732 to a more commodious building nearby, the theatre prospered under the vigorous management of Henry Giffard, an actor who took it over from Odell.[2] For this theatre, too, legal troubles were ahead.

Major changes in the older companies occurred during the seasons of 1732–3 and 1733–4. London gained a major new theatre when in December 1732 John Rich opened Covent Garden and transferred to it his company and his patent rights, retaining control of Lincoln's Inn Fields, however, which he thereafter used intermittently.[3] The location of Drury Lane did not change, but its management did—in consequence of the death or retirement of the actor-managers. Unlike Rich's patent

---

[1] See Emmett L. Avery, 'Foreign Performers in the London Theaters in the Early Eighteenth Century', *Philological Quarterly*, xvi (1937), 105–23; and Avery, 'The Defense and Criticism of Pantomimic Entertainment', loc. cit., pp. 127–45.

[2] Thomas Betterton, *A History of the English Stage* (London, 1741), p. 157; W. R. Chetwood, *A General History of the Stage* (London, 1749), p. 167. See also Watson Nicholson, *The Struggle for a Free Stage in London*, Ch. II; Arthur H. Scouten, *The London Stage, 1660–1800*, Part III (Carbondale, Ill., 1961), i. xxi–xxvii.

[3] It is not clear whether Lincoln's Inn Fields was operated by patent authority after Covent Garden was opened. John Rich held a dominant share in both the patents which Charles II had granted separately to Killigrew and D'Avenant; and according to a late eighteenth-century lawyer (Francis Hargrave) who investigated the matter in 1793 'there was a separate exercise of the two Patents for nearly ten Years together, namely, from 1732 to 1741 the late Mr. John Rich during that time keeping two Theatres open one at Covent Garden and the other in Lincoln's Inn Fields, without the least interruption or question from the Crown or any other Person—' (B.M. Add. MS. 12201, p. 3). Perhaps Hargrave was right; but it seems necessary to add that for the years in question Lincoln's Inn Fields was not generally recognized as a patent house.

For the season of 1736–7, Henry Giffard moved his company from Goodman's Fields to Lincoln's Inn Fields (Scouten, *London Stage*, ii. 597).

which was a grant in perpetuity, the Drury Lane patent was limited in its term to three years after the death of Steele—who had died on 1 September 1729.[1] In 1730 the actor-managers had applied successfully for a new patent, with a twenty-one-year term, which became effective precisely three years after Steele's death. As it happened, none of them personally exercised rights under it, but they or their heirs profited handsomely from it. Booth, who had been in poor health since 1727, sold half of his share during the summer of 1732 to John Highmore, a wealthy young man with more interest in than knowledge of the theatre. Wilks died soon after the new patent took effect, and his widow authorized a painter, John Ellys, to act as her representative in the management. Choosing to retire rather than serve with these new colleagues, Cibber rented his share for that season (1732-3) to his son Theophilus, a young man who was rapidly distinguishing himself for effrontery and irresponsibility.

The season under this heterogeneous group was as stormy as any in Drury Lane's long history—and the nature of it illuminates the confusion in theatrical law.[2] From the first Theophilus Cibber proved to be an overbearing and difficult colleague, especially since he had more experience in the theatre than Highmore and Ellys. For a time these two seem to have avoided trouble by allowing him to have his own way; but he became insufferable, and in an effort to have done with him Highmore in March 1733 bought at a high price his father's share in the patent. Theophilus did not peaceably submit to exclusion but began at once a clever and determined counterattack. In this he gained the co-operation of the company's principal actors, who formed an association, with Theophilus as head, in opposition to the patentees; and he further gained control of the Drury Lane lease.[3] He was thus able to demand harsh

[1] On the Drury Lane patent, see Loftis, *Steele at Drury Lane*, pp. 43-48.

[2] For detailed modern accounts of the season, see Barker, *Cibber*, Ch. IX; and Scouten, *London Stage*, I. lxxxix-xciii; for a good later eighteenth-century account, see Benjamin Victor, *The History of the Theatres of London and Dublin* (London, 1761), i. 3-31; for a biased but informative contemporary account, see 'A Letter from Theophilus Cibber, Comedian, to John Highmore, Esq.' (1733; copy in the British Museum).

[3] The actors' revolt led by Theophilus Cibber is the subject of a ballad opera performed at Covent Garden in July and August 1733: *The Stage Mutineers; Or, A Playhouse to Be Let*, 'By a Gentleman late of Trinity-College, Cambridge.' In this

terms from Highmore and Ellys—which they refused. When they also refused to surrender the theatre to him, his lease notwithstanding, he began legal proceedings to evict them; and in the interval he and his followers among the actors presented plays at Bartholomew Fair, during the summer, and at the Little Theatre in the Haymarket, in the autumn. Not having a patent (Theophilus had tried vainly to get one), the actors called themselves 'Comedians of His Majesty's Revels', a title apparently intended to disguise their anomalous legal status.

Their legal status was their vulnerable point, and it was consequently here that Highmore attacked them. Highmore gained reinforcement from John Rich, and together they took legal action (as managers of the two patent companies) not only against Theophilus Cibber's group at the Little Theatre in the Haymarket but also against the company in Goodman's Fields.[1] In form, their action was a charge of vagrancy directed against Henry Giffard of the latter theatre and John Mills of the former. This first effort failed on a legal technicality; but they tried again, this time singling out the comedian John Harper of the Haymarket, whom a Justice of the Peace did in fact commit to Bridewell. But their victory was short-lived, and further it cost them the good-will of the town. Theophilus Cibber was clever enough to represent the actors as the victims of legal oppression, and he won enthusiastic public support for them. On a subsequent hearing Harper was released, a circumstance of considerable legal significance in that it demonstrated the Court's unwillingness to support the theatrical monopolies represented in the patents. And when Theophilus gained physical possession of Drury Lane soon after, his victory over Highmore was complete. Highmore gave up and sold his share to another gentleman-amateur, John Fleetwood, with whom Theophilus soon came to terms advantageous to himself and to his fellow actors. Thus, in March 1734 the 'Comedians of His Majesty's Revels' were assimilated into the Drury Lane company.

This episode places in bold relief the ambiguity of the Government's attitude toward the theatres, and the confused state into

clever if inconsequential little piece, there are several humorous comparisons of theatrical and national politics, with suggestions of corruption in both.

[1] Nicholson, *Struggle for a Free Stage in London*, pp. 37-42; Barker, *Cibber*, pp. 171-3.

which the body of law controlling the theatres had fallen. Wilks, Booth, and Colley Cibber were granted the patent after the death of Steele because, in the words of a contemporary commentator, they 'were known to be long and well qualify'd for the Trust';[1] and yet they, or their heirs, promptly sold it, giving little attention to the capabilities of the buyers. The high prices that the shares in the patent brought (3,000 guineas for Cibber's third alone) bear witness to the current belief in the strength of theatrical monopoly. But the value of the patent rights depended on governmental support, i.e. the enforcing of the patentees' monopoly, and in the instance of Theophilus Cibber, this support was not forthcoming. To be sure, confidence that the patents would be protected seems to have persisted. The monopoly was challenged only in small and poorly equipped theatres, a circumstance which suggests that no one wished to risk the expense of opening a major theatre without the protection of a patent. Covent Garden was the only major theatre built in these years, and John Rich operated it under patent authority. But the ambiguity of the Government's attitude was sufficiently demoralizing for many people to desire clarification in it, even at the price of a limitation of freedom.[2]

Another sign—in addition to the rise of new theatres—that governmental control of the stage had weakened appears in the vagaries of censorship. When after 1715 the powers of the Master of the Revels were weakened (when Steele received his patent), the Lord Chamberlain sometimes acted in matters involving censorship, the most famous instance being the suppression of Gay's *Polly* in 1729.[3] In this affair, we hear nothing at all of a routine submission of the play for licensing when it was ready for rehearsal, although there was still a Master of the Revels in office; John Rich was summoned by the Lord Chamberlain's secretary and told that he must not rehearse any play until it

---

[1] *The Laureate; Or, The Right Side of Colley Cibber, Esq.* (London, 1740), p. 97.

[2] In commenting on the Licensing Act after describing these events of 1732-4, Benjamin Victor makes a helpful distinction between the authority granted to the Lord Chamberlain over the actors, which he regards as desirable, and the authority of the licenser over dramatic authors, which he regards as undesirable: *History of the Theatres*, i. 49-50.

[3] For an account of the office of the Master of the Revels in these years, see [John Genest], *Some Account of the English Stage* (Bath, 1832), iii. 23 ff.; White, 'The Office of Revels', loc. cit., pp. 23-25.

had been reviewed by the Lord Chamberlain. In a parallel instance, that of Walter Aston's *The Restoration of Charles II; Or, The Life and Death of Oliver Cromwell*, published in 1732, we again hear nothing of submission to the Master of the Revels. This time Potter, the proprietor of the Little Theatre in the Haymarket, required that the author obtain the approval of 'a Gentleman of the *Treasury*, and another of the *Exchequer*'.[1] This Aston was unable to do (presumably because the play could be suspected of Jacobite sympathies). In most cases of governmental interference in these years, action was taken *after* a play had been produced. We can be quite sure that the political plays staged by Henry Fielding in the 1730's had not undergone a licenser's critical review comparable to the careful reading that plays staged by Betterton and Christopher Rich the elder had been given in Queen Anne's reign.

The political scene was enlivened after the appearance of *The Beggar's Opera* by the offerings of the two 'little' theatres, the Little Theatre in the Haymarket and Goodman's Fields. The former seems to have been sympathetic to Walpole in the season of 1728-9,[2] defending him by way of satirical attacks on the opposition. John Mottley's *The Craftsman* in October satirized the journal of that name, its fictional author, Caleb D'Anvers, and the bumpkin squires who read it. The title of Thomas Odell's farce, *The Smugglers* (May 1729), suggests its subject. In his dedicatory epistle to 'George Doddington, *Esq*; One of the Lords Commissioners of His Majesty's Treasury', Odell writes so fully and so feelingly about the inequities arising from the widespread smuggling as to raise the suspicion that his farce was inspired by the Ministry.[3] Walpole's excise scheme was only a few years away. Together with the farce the Little Theatre produced Odell's ballad opera, *The Patron*, which seems to be rich in political innuendo, though the butt of its satire is not at all clear. Samuel Johnson of Cheshire's extravagant and nonsensical *Hurlothrumbo*, the most successful play of the season at the Haymarket, reveals no political theme in its printed

[1] Aston's Epistle 'To the Reader'.

[2] It nevertheless performed *The Beggar's Opera* during the season. Cf. Avery, *London Stage*, ii. 991 ff.

[3] That Walpole's Ministry was friendly to Odell is suggested by the fact that after the passage of the Licensing Act he became Deputy Licenser of Plays. *DNB*, s.v. Odell.

version—though actors may have interpolated improvised hits. At any rate, the play attracted the patronage of Sir Robert Walpole's son, Lord Walpole. If this be evidence of Walpole taste, we can see the point of the opposition predictions of a victory by the dunces.

The flirtation between the Little Theatre in the Haymarket and the Minister, if such indeed there was, came to an end the following season. No more plays appeared that were sympathetic to the Government or that were patronized by Walpole or his followers; rather, with Henry Fielding's *The Author's Farce* (March 1730) and *Tom Thumb* (April 1730) the theatre reached hesitantly to the opposition. On the surface little more political than Pope's *Dunciad* of 1728 (which it resembles), *The Author's Farce* is primarily a literary satire that has political implications and associations. These are latent in the fact that Wilks and Cibber appear in the play as at once types of the theatre manager and symbols of cultural corruption.[1] Already identified with the Ministry which in this year was to make him Laureate, Cibber was an established target for the opposition, who professed to see in his prominence a result of Walpole's corruption. The political meaning of *Tom Thumb* has remained an enigma.[2] Pamphlet and newspaper comment, which so often elucidates the political hits in plays of this era, gives no hint that contemporaries saw a double meaning in this one. Yet in view of the theatrical habits of these years, an implied and understood political meaning seems probable. Tom Thumb *the great*, the giant killer, the upholder of peace, the favourite of the queen, the successful lover—could all this be innocent of innuendo?

From these tentative forays into political satire, Fielding and the Little Theatre became much bolder in the season of 1730-1. *Tom Thumb* continued to be presented—in November with an interpolated interlude by someone other than Fielding, possibly Thomas Cooke, burlesquing the choice of Cibber as Poet Laureate;[3] and in March in Fielding's expanded version, *The*

---

[1] Dane F. Smith, *Plays about the Theatre in England from 'The Rehearsal' in 1671 to the Licensing Act in 1737* (New York and London, 1936), pp. 140–50; Sheridan Baker, 'Political Allusion in Fielding's *Author's Farce*, *Mock Doctor*, and *Tumble-Down Dick*', *PMLA*, lxxvii (1962), 221–31.

[2] See J. T. Hillhouse's account of the revisions of the play in his edition of it (New Haven, 1918), Introduction, pp. 9–10. Cf. Dudden, *Henry Fielding*, i. 66–69.

[3] See Loftis, *Comedy and Society from Congreve to Fielding*, p. 39.

Tragedy of Tragedies.[1] The spring of 1731 was a lively time at the theatre. If the political meaning of *The Tragedy of Tragedies* is mild and ambiguous, that of Fielding's *The Welsh Opera; Or, The Grey Mare the Better Horse* (April) is audacious and absolutely clear; this afterpiece in the form of ballad opera seems, in its rendering of Court gossip, to be a dramatization of Lord Hervey's *Memoirs*. Following performances of it in April, May, and June, Fielding tried to present a revised, sharpened, and lengthened version of the play, now called *The Grub-Street Opera*, but by this time the Government had had enough and suppressed it.[2] The play may have been performed in July, but there is no good evidence that it was. Its offensiveness to the Government is understandable enough, though it is non-partisan in the sense that both Walpole and his opponents are caricatured, and it is sufficiently genial to acknowledge allegorically Walpole's service to the nation. In its disguised but recognizable delineation of the King and Queen and above all in its allusions to the Prince of Wales's alleged impotence,[3] in this and in the more conventional review of Walpole's and Pulteney' shostility, it is bold even for the audacious decade of the 1730's.

In May (before Fielding revised this play), the Little Theatre in the Haymarket presented *The Fall of Mortimer*, a tragedy that was a scarcely disguised attack on the Government.[4] The authorship is understandably obscure, for it would have been a dangerous play to acknowledge. In its theme of a sovereign misled by an evil counsellor, who for his private gain subverts the constitutional rights of the people, it anticipates many opposition plays of the decade. Like later dramatic sovereigns this one is brought to an understanding of his servant's treachery by 'a Patriot Band',

Those Guardian Angels of a sinking Land [the prologue explains],
Deploring their lov'd Country's wretched State,
Bravely resolv'd to snatch her from her Fate.

[1] Wilbur L. Cross, *The History of Henry Fielding* (New Haven, 1918), i. 97–102.
[2] Jack Richard Brown, 'Henry Fielding's *Grub-Street Opera*', *Modern Language Quarterly*, xvi (1955), 32–41. Cf. Genest, *English Stage*, iii. 323; Cross, *Fielding*, i. 111; and Dudden, *Fielding*, i. 90.
[3] On this subject, see Hervey, *Memoirs*, ed. Sedgwick, ii. 614–18.
[4] *The Craftsman*, 8 May 1731, calls *The Fall of Mortimer* 'An historical PLAY, alter'd from Edward III of Mountfort'. However, the attribution of *Edward III* to Mountfort may be an error (cf. Nicoll, *Restoration Drama*, p. 388).

The followers of Pulteney and Bolingbroke must have found much to cheer in the crude and very direct allegory of this piece, in which Mortimer, chief counsellor of the young King Edward III, supported by the Queen Mother, exercises a tyrannical control over the nation's affairs. ''Tis full three Years', says one of the patriots, in a covert reference to George II's reinstatement of Walpole after his accession (1):

> since *Mortimer*
> Began to lord it o'er us by the Queen's vile Favour.

The favourite's fall comes when the young king, educated by the patriots, arrives at an understanding of his prerogative. All this was too blatant to be tolerated for long, and when, after a grand jury in July delivered a presentment against the play (and against several pamphlets and articles in *The Craftsman*), the company attempted to perform it, a high constable came to the theatre to arrest the actors. They contrived to escape on this occasion, but they were harassed by the Government later in the summer, even for producing such a seemingly innocuous play as *Hurlothrumbo*.[1]

The following season the management of the Little Theatre grew more cautious. Fielding took his new plays to Drury Lane, and thus was no longer an irritant. Samuel Johnson tried another piece of nonsense in March 1732, *The Blazing Comet*, this time without success. It was at the end of this season that Potter, the theatre's manager, insisted that Walter Aston secure governmental approval in advance for his opera, *The Restoration of King Charles II*. As we have seen, the play was not approved, and Aston's petulant dedication of the published play to Walpole reveals a sense of oppression.

The second 'little' theatre, Goodman's Fields, exhibited no very clear political bias. With Thomas Odell as its first manager and Henry Giffard as a prominent actor and subsequent manager, both of whom gave evidence of 'loyalty' to the Government,[2] we would expect it to avoid attacks on Walpole. Yet Goodman's Fields produced an opposition play in its first season (1729–30), *The Fate of Villainy*, attributed to Thomas Walker,[3]

---

[1] Cross, *Fielding*, i. 111–12.
[2] On Odell, see p. 103, n. 3 above; on Giffard, see Scouten, *London Stage*, i. lxxxii–lxxxiv.
[3] Nicoll, *Early Eighteenth Century Drama*, p. 363.

and another one in its second season, *The Fall of the Earl of Essex*, an adaptation by James Ralph from a tragedy of John Banks. However, the tone of both plays differs from that of *The Fall of Mortimer*. To be sure, the dramatists again portray courtiers who abuse the confidence of their sovereigns to commit treacherous acts—but imagination is required to identify the courtiers with Walpole. *The Fate of Villainy*, which is a tragedy of complex court intrigue set in the kingdom of Aragon, suggests English affairs merely in its depiction of a corrupt minister's usurpation of powers that are properly regal. Because the favourite depicted in *The Fall of the Earl of Essex* is sheltered by a queen, in this instance Queen Elizabeth, his situation is somewhat more analogous to Walpole's, who enjoyed the confidence of Queen Caroline; and there are particulars in the charges made against Essex which in 1731 would have sounded like an arraignment of Walpole. Thus Lord Burleigh's remarks to Queen Elizabeth hint at Walpole's peace policy (1):

> Your *Essex* who betray'd his Charge,—forgot
> The use of Arms, commens'd a Truce against
> Your absolute Command; who parley'd oft,
> In secret, with the Rebel Chief, ev'n like
> A Monarch exercis'd his Pow'r in Peace,
> But like a beaten Coward in the Field—

The propagandistic blows were indirect, but they were none the less effective, and they were not so vulnerable to governmental interference.

The opposition received support not only from the little theatres, but from Lincoln's Inn Fields as well. John Rich showed restraint in the plays he produced—he clearly wished to avoid trouble—but several of them had political overtones that could not be misunderstood. A prologue spoken before a revival in 1729 of Brady's *The Rape* sounds the 'Patriot' denunciation of Walpole's peace policy, and in the same year Samuel Madden's *Themistocles, the Lover of His Country* turned Greek history to political service. Dedicated to the Prince of Wales, who had recently arrived in England, *Themistocles* has a prologue that points the moral which the play was to inculcate, a moral at that time preached by the opposition:

> Taught by these Scenes, espouse your Country's Cause,
> Renounce your Factions, and revere your Laws! . . .

Act not from servile Views of Power, or Place;
Preferr'd, be Just, or Loyal in Disgrace.

Again, George Jeffrey's *Merope* (1731) includes lines in celebration of patriotism and liberty that would have had a specialized meaning.

So long as Cibber and his fellow actor-managers were in control of Drury Lane, that theatre, in contrast with the Little Theatre in the Haymarket, Goodman's Fields, and Lincoln's Inn Fields, did not present plays patently hostile to Walpole. Yet Drury Lane cannot be said to have actively supported Walpole or his policies. The only plays of any political audacity produced there in the last years of the triumvirate, Benjamin Martyn's *Timoleon* (1730) and David Mallet's *Eurydice* (1731), hark back to England's dynastic problems, and it is questionable whether Mallet's play does even this much. *Timoleon* is emphatically a Hanoverian play; *Eurydice* just possibly a Jacobite one.[1]

Mallet's *Eurydice* first appeared at Drury Lane on 22 February 1731. Some six weeks earlier, on 13 January, a tragedy on virtually the same subject appeared at Lincoln's Inn Fields.

---

[1] It is clear that *Timoleon* is essentially an allegorical justification of the right of revolution as the Whigs understood it to apply to the Revolution of 1688, and that Timoleon is to be identified with William III. To be sure, Martyn dedicated the play to George II, tactfully suggesting that he served as model for the exemplary protagonist; but the violent course of the play itself, in which Timoleon acquiesces in the deposition and even the assassination of his sovereign and brother, is far closer to William's experience.

A few lines from the prologue may conceal innuendo of an opposition bias:

Attentive then the Grecian Patriot view,
While, strict the Paths of Virtue to pursue,
Nor Love, nor Friendship, nor the Ties of Blood
Abate his Ardor for the publick Good.

The use of the word 'Patriot', the allusion to a political disinterestedness extending to a refusal of partiality to one's kinsmen, the invocation of a magnanimous public spirit—all of this may have had a double meaning. That it did so is implied by a contemporary pamphleteer (*Remarks on the Tragedy of Timoleon* [London, n.d.], pp. 24-25).

As for Mallet's play, we have the suggestion of a pamphleteer (*Remarks on the Tragedy of Eurydice* [London, 1731], pp. 6-9) that Mallet wrote it as Jacobite propaganda on the suggestion of 'an eminent Hand, remarkable for great Parts...', who made use of the other as a Tool in the Matter, without letting him into any part of his Intention'. Bolingbroke presumably was meant; Mallet later served as his literary executor. However, it is difficult to discover any evidence for the charge of Jacobitism in the play itself, which is not propagandistic but rather a serious and semi-successful effort at neoclassical tragedy.

But John Tracy's *Periander*, unlike *Eurydice*, is blatantly a propaganda play, providing clear evidence of John Rich's political leanings. (It can scarcely be coincidence that two tragedies on the same episode in Greek history appeared within such a short span of time; since Tracy's play is clumsy as well as propagandistic, I would surmise that it was written after news of Mallet's was abroad, in an effort to anticipate him.)

The prologue of *Periander* sounds familiar opposition notes and in effect establishes the theme of the tragedy to follow. Among the *dramatis personae* are Zeno and Alcander, 'Two of the greatest Men in Corinth, Conspiring to restore the ancient Form of Government', who may be identified with Pulteney and Bolingbroke. In an introductory and expository conversation, these two review the condition of Corinth under the tyrant Periander, describing political abuses and atrocities that were the conventional specifications in the arraignment of Walpole. Alcander regrets the spread of enervating luxury, which plunges the nation 'in Sloth, in Poverty,/In Guilt, Corruption, Slavery and Ruin'; and in this play produced just ten years after Walpole became Chancellor of the Exchequer, he pledges that

> We, like our *Grecian* Ancestors of old,
> Will in our glorious Course unweary'd hold.
> Tho' ten long Years our great Design retard,
> Freedom at last will be a full Reward.

This is explicit enough to have raised opposition cheers.

The journalistic criticism of Drury Lane and Lincoln's Inn Fields continued to be calibrated to their political differences. In the years following the production of *The Beggar's Opera*, Drury Lane—for all its shortcomings—provided a better and more consistent diet of serious drama competently produced than any other London theatre. Yet in Mist's *Weekly Journal*, Applebee's *Weekly Journal*, *The Craftsman*, and *The Grub-Street Journal*, all in opposition to Drury Lane as well as to Walpole, there is little acknowledgement of its achievements. It would seem that hatred for Walpole and for everybody associated with him made a fair appraisal of the theatre's merits impossible.

Virtually the only journal to indicate an awareness of Drury Lane's artistic accomplishment was one sympathetic to Walpole,

The Comedian,[1] conducted by Thomas Cooke. In an essay[2] (October 1732) occasioned by the death of Robert Wilks, Cooke by way of an obituary briefly reviews Wilks's career and at more length the state of the theatres. He has forthright praise for the perennial butt, the Poet Laureate: 'The elder *Cibber* is, even by the Confession of his Enemys, a Comedian eminent in many Walks, an Excellence in any one of which would give a Player an extraordinary Character; nor is he to be excluded the first Class of comic Writers.' And he praises the lesser actors of the company: Johnson, Griffin, Harper, Theophilus Cibber, Mills, Mrs. Booth, Mrs. Cibber, and Mrs. Raftor, among others. Cooke mentions that political touchstone *The Beggar's Opera* as 'a truly reasonable entertaining Piece, and a just and good Satire on a prevailing ridiculous Taste', but he deplores the fact that 'it has given Birth to Rubbish more absurd than the Operas on which it is a Satire'. Of its political satire, he says not a word; indeed, throughout the essay he passes no judgement that can be attributed with confidence to political bias. His sharpest criticism, to be sure, is reserved for John Rich, but the reason for it is the usual one with serious dramatic critics—Rich's sponsorship of 'non-rational' spectacle.

The Grub-Street Journal, a periodical of important literary associations, reveals an obvious hostility to Drury Lane and a somewhat less obvious hostility to the Hanoverians and to Walpole.[3] It originated (in 1730) as essentially a continuation of Pope's *Dunciad*; it understandably shares Pope's opinion of Cibber, ultimately king of the dunces, and of Drury Lane, a conspicuous seat of 'dullness', and shares also Pope's political views on the infrequent occasions when it touches political topics. During most of its run, however, it was independent of Pope. Since it printed letters from persons with conflicting literary and dramatic interests, it expresses no single, consistent attitude toward the theatres, the personnel of which, moreover, underwent several major changes during the journal's life (1730–7). Still, it reveals some abiding attitudes in theatrical commentary that imply patterns of political association.

---

[1] *The Comedian*, No. 3 (June 1732), includes a poem praising Walpole.

[2] Reprinted in Loftis (ed.), *Essays on the Theatre from Eighteenth-Century Periodicals*, pp. 6–10.

[3] For a comprehensive discussion of this periodical, see James T. Hillhouse, *The Grub-Street Journal* (Durham, N.C., 1928).

Most conspicuous, as with Mist's, is the disdain for Cibber. His odes produced in line of duty as Poet Laureate were submitted to a mock-serious critique, and the abundant weaknesses of his prose were gleefully exposed. Because he was an able comic actor, not much could be made of his usual performances on the stage beyond insinuations that little acting was necessary for him to play the role of a fop, but when he made his ill-advised appearances in tragic parts he exposed himself to laughter. Quite apart from political considerations, Cibber was a 'dunce' in Pope's sense of the term and hence fair game; and yet the overt and continuing hostility of the journal, the political bias of which was Tory and Jacobite,[1] is meaningful when directed to a man signally distinguished by the Walpole Government.

This is further confirmed by the journal's more kindly treatment of John Rich. If willing to print isolated contributions favourable to Cibber and to Drury Lane and conversely hostile to Rich, the journal revealed on the whole greater sympathy for him. The correspondent who called himself 'Somebody', who was supported editorially and over a protracted period given liberal space, defended Rich (displaying while doing so an intimate knowledge of his affairs) when Rich was attacked by another correspondent, possibly Colley Cibber himself, who used the pseudonym 'No-body'.[2] Rich received this support, it has been suggested,[3] more because of his rivalry with the Cibbers, Colley and Theophilus, than because of any admiration the journal's authors felt for Rich himself.

Rich's production of Gay's *Achilles* in February 1733 (after Gay's death) at the new Covent Garden Theatre brought journalistic comment which followed political lines. This burlesque of a classical fable seems innocent enough,[4] but any play by Gay would have been hateful to the Walpole group. *The Daily Courant*, 16 February 1733, faithful to the Government,

---

[1] Cf. ibid., pp. 6–7 n.   [2] Ibid., pp. 210–14.
[3] Ibid., p. 213.
[4] A pamphlet appeared in 1733 with the following title: *Achilles Dissected: Being a Complete Key of the Political Characters in that New Ballad Opera, Written by the Late Mr. Gay. An Account of the Plan upon Which It Was Founded. With Remarks upon the Whole.* 'By Mr. Burnett.' (Nicoll, *Early Eighteenth Century Drama*, p. 241 n., says that it was allegedly written by Guthry.) The pamphlet is an inconsequential parody of efforts to find political meaning in plays.

devoted one of its rare dramatic essays to a forthright deprecia-
tion of it; whereas *The Grub-Street Journal*, 22 February 1733,
characteristically siding against Walpole and with Pope's friends,
printed a reply. Even before the play was performed Applebee's *Weekly Journal*, 20 January 1733, still hostile to Walpole,
puffed it; and a week after its first performance *The Craftsman*,
17 February 1733, included an appreciative notice.

In the years of Walpole's dominance only *The Prompter* included sustained and informed discussion of the drama and of
theatrical problems that is largely free of political colouring.
Conducted by Aaron Hill and William Popple from 1734 to
1736, it was a distinguished periodical, the first English journal
with an extended run to be primarily devoted to the theatre.[1]
Only *The Tatler*, *The Spectator*, and *The Guardian* had previously
contained theatrical criticism comparable in extent and quality
—and they too had largely been free of politics. In other journals non-political essays or groups of essays about the theatre
appeared from time to time; but in relation to the bulk of early
eighteenth-century periodical publication there are surprisingly
few of them.

Politics and gossip both provided matter for pamphlets in
dramatic and ballad opera form in the early 1730's. *The Beggar's
Opera*, Lord Hervey said in his *Memoirs*, 'was thought to reflect
a little upon the Court',[2] presumably in its depiction of the
family relationships of the Peachums; and gossip about the royal
family, especially the Prince of Wales, of the kind dramatized by
Fielding in *The Grub-Street Opera* seems to have provided sport
for a number of less talented writers. Only nominally dramatic,
such plays were not acted and probably were not intended to
be; they are interesting chiefly for the glimpses they provide,
through a transparent curtain of fiction, of famous people and
their affairs. For example, *Mr. Taste, the Poetical Fop; Or, The
Modes of the Court* (1732) has as its title character one who is as
easily recognized today as he was in the eighteenth century:
'Mr. *Alexander Taste*, A Poet who, in spite of deformity, imagines
every Woman he sees in love with him, and imprudently makes

---

[1] For discussion of *The Prompter*, see Brewster, *Aaron Hill*, pp. 122–39; and Gray,
Theatrical Criticism in London to 1795, pp. 87–97.

[2] Ed., Sedgwick, i. 98.

Addresses to *Lady Airy*.' And in other plays we have renderings of the famous story, told at length by Hervey, of the Prince of Wales's courtship of Miss Vane.[1]

While in 1733 the Court was enlivened by the intrigues of the Prince of Wales, and the theatres by the scheming of Theophilus Cibber, the politicians were preoccupied with Walpole's Excise Bill—a measure which aroused such a vigorous resistance that Walpole was forced to withdraw it after the second reading.[2] The Bill proposed the use of bonded warehouses in the wine and tobacco trade as storage places for imported goods, re-exportation to be permitted duty free, and excise duty to be charged on the commodities sold for domestic consumption. The scheme was intended at once to make the machinery of tax collecting more efficient and to spread the tax burden more equitably. But the Bill did not pass, because the opposition, playing on the public fears of a general excise (a tax on the consumption of all commodities) and of the officials who would be charged with collecting the duties, succeeded in raising a strident cry of protest. In disseminating their propaganda, they turned to the drama.

As I have suggested, the denunciations of excise in dramatic form were not intended for the stage nor did they appear. They were too forthright in their criticism of the Minister even for the theatres of that outspoken decade. In *The Honest Electors* Walpole is 'Sir Positive Screenall, a conceited, foolish, blundering

---

[1] *Vanelia; Or, The Amours of the Great* (1732) includes a broad treatment of the Miss Vane, Lord Hervey, Prince of Wales affair, with a satirical review of the Sir Robert Walpole and Molly Skerritt relationship added for good measure. *The Humours of the Court; Or, Modern Gallantry* (1732) again depicts the Vane–Hervey–Prince of Wales triangle; and it also includes a character, Captain Modish, 'a rakish Officer, with a good Assurance, Confidant to Adonis [the Prince of Wales]', who would seem to represent Captain Bodens, the putative author of a comedy, *The Modish Couple*, presented at Drury Lane in January 1732, which was, in all probability, the result of a collaboration by the Prince of Wales and Lord Hervey. (Charles B. Woods, 'Captian B——'s Play', *Harvard Studies and Notes in Philology and Literature*, xv [1933], 243–55.) Still another dramatization of the famous triangle was published as an interlude in *The Modish Couple* itself: *The Promised Marriage; Or, The Disappointed Lady*. We may be sure that these little pieces abound with innuendo, easily understood in the early eighteenth century, which is now lost to us.

[2] On the Excise Bill, see E. R. Turner, 'The Excise Scheme of 1733', *English Historical Review*, xlii (1927), 34–57; A. J. Henderson, *London and the National Government, 1721–1742* (Durham, N.C., 1945), Ch. VI; and J. H. Plumb, *Sir Robert Walpole: The King's Minister*, Ch. VII.

M- - - - - -r'; in *The State Juggler* he is 'Sir Politick Ribband'; in *Rome Excised* he is '*Cyrenius*', favourite of Augustus Caesar and 'a Promoter of unprecedented Taxes'. A statement by a Roman senator in this last play will suggest not only its theme but the theme of this entire group of political tracts in dramatic form (1):

This general Tax, if ratify'd by the *Senate* and *Augustus*, will bring Oppression upon us all, and may hereafter prove a Precedent for worse, if worse can be; and will not then Posterity have Cause to curse us, if we tamely acquiesce, and use not our utmost Efforts to prevent its Progress? 'tis the Project of *Cyrenius*, who, not content with what he has already done, will lop the Growth of Arts and Sciences, and bring us all to Slavery.

In the plays I have named and in at least three more, *The Court Legacy*,[1] *The Commodity Excised*, and *The Sturdy Beggars*, all of them in the ballad opera form that five years after Gay's success still seemed appropriate to the opposition, Walpole and his excise scheme are denounced as menaces to British liberties.

Although none of the plays produced had hits at the Excise Bill included in their texts, we may be sure that the theatres in this decade resounded to political innuendo, conveyed by words and phrases interpolated in prepared dialogue, and by tone and inflexion of voice in the delivery of lines, which in print would seem innocent enough. We hear for example of a pantomime presented in March 1733 at the Little Theatre in the Haymarket, in which remarks unfavourable to the Bill were inserted. Walpole's son was in the audience and reacted vigorously, as we learn from Applebee's *Weekly Journal*, 31 March 1733:

On Thursday 7-Night last at the Performance of the Pantomime Entertainment call'd Love runs all Dangers, at the New Theatre in the Hay-Market, one of the Commedians took the Liberty to throw out some Reflections upon the Prime Minister and the Excise, which were not design'd by the Author; Lord Walpole being in the House, went behind the Scenes, and demanded of the Prompter, whether such Words were in the Play, and he answering they were not, his Lordship immediately corrected the Comedian with his own Hands very severely.

Fragmentary as our information in this instance may be, the

---

[1] On this play see Edmund McAdoo Gagey, *Ballad Opera* (New York, 1937), p. 185. (I have not examined the play.)

episode suggests the heat of tempers in this year of the Excise, and it also suggests the difficulty of effective governmental supervision as the theatres were then constituted.

The cry against Walpole as sounded in comedy and ballad opera in the 1730's characteristically assumed the form of denunciation of corruption: of corruption either in a specific political sense or in a more generalized social sense. By reason of the long repetition of charges against the Minister of peculation, manipulation of elections, bribery, and infringement of constitutional liberties, even the briefest allusion to these crimes (or merely to unspecified 'corruption') implied a hit at Walpole.

Even before Walpole came to first place in the Ministry, the manipulation of rural elections, so widely practised in that borough-mongering age, had been subjected to dramatic satire by Mrs. Centlivre, whose *The Gotham Election* was published in 1715 after the Master of the Revels had refused permission for it to be acted.[1] We hear again of corruption in rural elections in several plays of the 1730's. A person who called himself 'Mark Freeman' published in 1733 *The Downfall of Bribery; Or, The Honest Men of Taunton*, a political tract in ballad opera form which dramatizes an episode described succinctly in *The Craftsman*, 24 November 1733: 'A few Persons at TAUNTON, who had it in their Power to turn the Election of a *Mayor*, lately refused a Sum of TWO THOUSAND POUNDS for their Votes, upon that Occasion.' But it was Fielding who realized the full comic potential in the rural traffic in votes. In his *Don Quixote in England* (1734), and perhaps also in his *Pasquin* (1736), both produced at the Little Theatre in the Haymarket, he went beyond propaganda to achieve comedy. He handled the subject boisterously, with an implied acknowledgement that the Country party was not above adroit manoeuvring of its own; but his comedies were nevertheless well calculated to serve the ends of the opposition and *Pasquin* at least had a huge success.[2]

Fielding was more specific in depicting corruption than most of the dramatists, who in the main contented themselves with observations on the power of gold to corrupt. Thus John Kelly

[1] John Wilson Bowyer, *The Celebrated Mrs. Centlivre* (Durham, N.C., 1952), p. 161.
[2] Cf. Laprade, *Public Opinion and Politics*, pp. 376-7.

in an interesting adaptation from de l'Isle, *Timon in Love* (Drury Lane, 1733), uses mythological characters and a situation that owes something to Apuleius to make moralistic comments having a political edge. Timon accompanied by his ass goes on a pilgrimage in search of enlightenment; and when the ass is miraculously granted the power of speech the two of them discuss the society surrounding them in a vein suggestive of *The Dunciad* and *Gulliver's Travels*. The ballad operas that for some nine years after 1728 continued to appear in large numbers[1] frequently echo Gay's observations on gold and bribery. So in *The Mock Lawyer* (Covent Garden, 1733) a song begins (p. 24) 'There is nothing but Feeing in Fashion,' and in *The Lover His Own Rival* (Goodman's Fields, 1736) one begins (p. 17) 'The Power of Gold does all others surpass.' Satire of Walpole had become a stylized convention, and consequently could be accomplished economically and unobtrusively.

The opposition represented, in the contemporary terminology, the Country party; and in their principal journal *The Craftsman* the leaders of the opposition made capital of their association with the country squires of England. The contrast between town and country had long provided comedies with themes; characters appeared representing town and country manners, and they often debated the rival advantages of rural and urban life. In the earlier years of the century, as throughout the later years of the seventeenth century, the dramatists (with a few exceptions such as Farquhar and Charles Johnson) had revealed in their implied evaluations a marked preference for town life. After *The Beggar's Opera*, however, with its jovial yet damning depiction of life in London's underworld, we notice a growing affection displayed in comedy and ballad opera for rural England;[2] and it is an affection that is often associated with hatred of Walpole. Urban corruption, in *The Beggar's Opera* and in many imitations of it, becomes a prime symbol of the corruption of Walpole's England; and beautiful rural England becomes the corollary symbol of the uncorrupted part of the nation. Fielding's plays as well as his novels show this revision of the earlier values, and so do many obscure plays of the 1730's, notably the dramatic entertainments at Drury Lane by Robert Dodsley, *The King*

---

[1] For a comprehensive account of them, see Gagey, *Ballad Opera*.

[2] Loftis, *Comedy and Society from Congreve to Fielding*, pp. 103-8.

and the Miller of Mansfield (1737) and *Sir John Cockle at Court* (1738); and often, as with Fielding and Dodsley, the preference for country over town is accompanied by support for the Country party.

Walpole's opponents seem to have been much more active in the theatres than his friends. There may have been some factual basis for the satirical representation, in *The Daily Gazetteer,* 14 April 1737,[1] of Lord Lyttelton as enlisting dramatists in the service of the opposition. Certainly with Pulteney, Bolingbroke, Chesterfield, and Lyttelton as directors of opposition propaganda, there was no lack of organization, talent, and money to animate it. Occasionally we hear querulous notes from dramatists who resented the opposition's vigour. William Popple's complaint in the preface to his *The Lady's Revenge* (Covent Garden, 1734) suggests the power of Walpole's enemies in the theatres: 'A Report having been maliciously raised, and industriously spread all over the Town, that the Play was a Party Play, and supported by the Court, and therefore to be opposed, Numbers of Persons came into the House with an Intent, (as the Term is) to damn it at all Events.' The play does indeed seem to be politically innocent. One of the few attempts to score a hit at the opposition appears in John Hewitt's *A Tutor for the Beaus* (Lincoln's Inn Fields, 1737), a play significantly dedicated to 'Miss Skerret', Walpole's mistress and later his second wife. 'Instead of passing three Quarters of their Lives in a Coffee-House', says Lord Modely (1), a fop who has recently come from Paris, 'poring over *Gazettes,* and murdering Politics, they [the English] wou'd do much better, if they saw good Company at home. . . .' (This was apparently intended as good advice, even if spoken by a fool.) By comparison to the hits at Walpole, the counterblows struck in his behalf were weak indeed.

The most comprehensive dramatic review of the political machinations of the late 1730's, and one which is largely impartial, appears in a curious play by Francis Lynch, *The Independent Patriot* (Lincoln's Inn Fields, 1737). Lynch claims in his dedication to the Earl of Burlington that his subject is new, that in writing the play he borrowed nothing from predecessors;

[1] Cited in Rose Mary Davis, *The Good Lord Lyttelton* (Bethlehem, Pa., 1939), p. 54.

and it is true that the play has in its unconventionality of characterization and plot development and in its fullness of unex-
pected detail many of the qualities we associate with the novel
rather than the drama. It depicts the London political world of
scheming and counterscheming, apparently giving us a sampling
of current political conversation. The character 'Medium' is the
'Independent Patriot' of the title—emphasis should be placed
on the adjective rather than the noun, for the character, who
is a member of Parliament, is critical of the opposition as well
as of Walpole. 'I voted with the Minister,' he explains (1), 'as
I shall whenever I think him in the right—I never differ'd with
him out of Pique or Prejudice.' Elsewhere there is virtually
a parody of opposition talk. Sanguine, 'a nominal Patriot',
speaks (1):

Damn all Ribbands that shou'd seduce a Man from the Interest
of his Country!—My Curse on the first Inventors of Badges and Titles!
They've done *England* more real Injury than her religious Hypocrites. 'Tis strange, and yet 'tis too true, my Friend; that Shreds of
Blue, Green and Red have injur'd old *England* more essentially than
all her Wars with *France*.

Yet we learn that Sanguine, who speaks thus vehemently, is
secretly in Walpole's employ and merely pretends allegiance to
the opposition to learn their secrets. Scattered through the play
there are strong and forthright hits at Walpole's policy of
maintaining good relations with the French; and there are hits
both at his use of appointments as bribes and at opposition
susceptibility to such bribes. The inept dialogue of the play notwithstanding, it has a certain documentary interest as an effort
at an impartial portrait of the political manners of the time.

Tragedy of the 1730's bears the impress of opposition propaganda scarcely less plainly than comedy; and in tragedy as in
comedy the attacks on Walpole follow clear and recurrent
patterns. There are in brief two major patterns, the exemplary
and the cautionary: the depiction of admirable statesmen who
are conspicuous for the qualities Walpole allegedly lacked; and
the depiction of despicable statesmen who exhibit the traits of
personality or of policy with which he was habitually charged.
In these tense years few tragedies appeared that would not bear
a double interpretation, whether intended by the author or not.

Because tragedy depicted persons in high places in actions that led to catastrophe, it lent itself to closer, more literal application to Walpole and his circumstances, at least as the opposition wished them to be, than did comedy.

In so far as this political theory is coherent, it is that to which Bolingbroke gave systematic exposition in his *Idea of a Patriot King*, first published years after the Licensing Act but known in preliminary statements much earlier.[1] Bolingbroke was a leading spirit of the opposition until 1735, and we know enough of his eloquence and personal charm to be sure that his political opinions gained a wide hearing in conversation. He both wrote for and supervised opposition publications, including *The Craftsman*; and he cultivated poets, notably Pope and Thomson, who lent the force of their high talent to the expression of his partisan views.[2] With his eye fixed on Frederick, Prince of Wales, he urged a lofty conception of constitutional monarchy, in which the king would use his royal prerogative to regain powers the Ministers had usurped and would reanimate his people to a jealous concern for the preservation of their liberties. All this assumed an able and unselfish king, who would in effect act as his own Prime Minister; and Bolingbroke, Lyttelton, and Pitt attempted to convey an impression of the Prince of Wales as well equipped for such a role. They were supported by a number of tragic dramatists, who searched history for instances of kings reasserting their prerogative and ridding themselves of courtiers who diminished royal authority.

I have already mentioned several such tragedies produced in 1730 and 1731—*The Fall of the Earl of Essex*, *The Fate of Villainy*, and *The Fall of Mortimer*—all of them portraying the career of a royal favourite who, having abused his power, meets a deserved end at the hands of an aroused sovereign. And there were other tragedies later in the decade cut to the same pattern, though they were not all produced on the stage. Perhaps the grossest of the admonitions in tragic form to Walpole and his

[1] Mabel Hessler Cable, '*The Idea of a Patriot King* in the Propaganda of the Opposition to Walpole, 1735-1739', *Philological Quarterly*, xviii (1939), 119-30.
[2] A. D. McKillop, 'Ethics and Political History in Thomson's *Liberty*', in *Pope and His Contemporaries: Essays Presented to George Sherburn*, ed. James L. Clifford and Louis A. Landa (Oxford, 1949), pp. 215-29; and McKillop, *The Background of Thompson's 'Liberty'* (Rice Institute Pamphlets, vol. xxxiii, No. ii, Houston, 1951), Ch. VII.

sovereign (or sovereign-to-be) is *Majesty Misled; Or, The Over-throw of Evil Ministers* (1734), 'As intended to be Acted at one of the Theatres, But was refus'd for CERTAIN REASONS.' In fact, so obvious are the allegorical strictures on Walpole and even on the King that the play could scarcely have been intended for presentation on the stage. Dedicated to a recent Lord Mayor of London who had opposed the Excise Bill, the tragedy depicts the disasters that resulted when Edward II, 'A weak Prince, misguided by his depraved Favourites', allowed the two Spencers, father and son, to usurp powers that the Sovereign alone should exercise.

A more interesting treatment of the theme of 'majesty mis-led' appears in William Havard's *King Charles the First*, pro-duced at Lincoln's Inn Fields in 1737 in a form more innocuous politically than that in which it was published. As is explained in the preface of the published play, certain marked lines were omit-ted in the acted version; and these lines are invariably ones that emphasize the parallels between Charles I's reign and George II's. Havard establishes in lines that were spoken on the stage by a normative character, Fairfax, his attitude toward the con-stitutional problems inherent in his subject—in the deposition and death of Charles (i):

> *Charles* grasp'd, we own, at Arbitrary Sway,
> And wou'd have been a Tyrant—for which Crime
> The Kingdoms he was born to, we have seiz'd:
> But let us not despoil him of his Life.
> Crowns as the Gift of Men, Men may resume,
> But Life, the Gift of Heaven, let Heaven dispose of.

Having made thus explicit his political assumptions, Havard explores the causes and implications of Charles's destruction, and in doing so points a moral to George II, who, like Charles, had retained his father's Ministers. In lines omitted in stage production (ii), a character (Cromwell) pointedly alludes to Charles's having kept a Minister despite his monopoly of govern-mental power, his use of money stolen from the public treasury to buy popularity, and his refusal to protect English shipping from piratical foreigners. Yet the tragedy is not merely a propa-ganda piece but has pretensions to literary form.

Even many of the celebrations of political liberty were partisan. In the preliminaries of his burlesque *The Covent-Garden*

Tragedy (1732) Fielding ironically alludes to the political clichés of tragedy, most of which may be associated with the opposition programme:

> The first five Lines are mighty pretty Satyr on our Age, our Country, Statesmen, Lawyers, and Physicians: What did I not expect from such a Beginning? But alas! what follows? No fine Moral Sentences, not a Word of Liberty and Property, no Insinuations, that Courtiers are Fools, and Statesmen Rogues. You have indeed a few Similies, but they are very thin sown.

The omissions in *The Covent-Garden Tragedy* are amply compensated for by surpluses in other plays. The dramatists searched for and found historical figures who symbolized the defence of 'liberty and property'. The fact that the career of George Castriot, called Scanderbeg, King of Epirus and Albania, provided the basis for three tragedies in the space of a few years may be attributed to its usefulness as a symbol of resistance to tyranny. William Havard's *Scanderbeg* was produced at Goodman's Fields in 1733; George Lillo's *The Christian Hero* at Drury Lane in 1735; and Thomas Whincop's *Scanderbeg* was published posthumously in 1747, having been written much earlier.[1] Of these Lillo's *The Christian Hero* most clearly served the ends of the opposition, its production at the Theatre Royal in Drury Lane notwithstanding. Havard's play, despite its subject, gives greater emphasis to love intrigue than to political action; and Whincop's did not gain an audience until after Walpole's fall. Lillo concentrates on the political lessons to be learned: the wrongness of tyranny and usurpation of power, and the rightness of the defence of sacred honour in battle. Lest there be uncertainty about his themes, Lillo provides a gloss on them in his prologue and epilogue. 'To Night we sing/A Pious Hero, and a Patriot King' goes the prologue, this last phrase in its identity with the title of Bolingbroke's treatise suggesting the origin of Lillo's ideas:

> By Nature form'd, by Providence design'd
> To scourge Ambition, and to right Mankind.

The epilogue enunciates Bolingbroke's ideal of a monarchy free from faction:

[1] In the preface to Whincop's *Scanderbeg* Lillo is accused of taking the theme of his play from Whincop's (Nicoll, *Early Eighteenth Century Drama*, p. 84.)

What if each Briton, in his Private Station,
Should try to bilk those, who imbroil the Nation;
Quit either Faction, and, like Men, unite
To do their King and injured Country Right.

The appeal to Englishmen—both here and in Bolingbroke's
writings—to rise above party meant for them to throw out
Walpole.

As so often in the England of the seventeenth and eighteenth
centuries Roman history provided episodes to point a political
moral. The conception of the 'patriot' as it was reinterpreted
for opposition use had as its central ingredient the ideal of the
disinterested Roman lover of liberty, of which Addison's *Cato*
is the classic English expression. (And it is notable that the play
was called upon again to do party service; Lord Hervey
describes the Prince of Wales at a performance of *Cato* in 1737,
cheering with the opposition.[1]) Two of the celebrations of 'Freedom, and Independency from Power' appeared in new dramatizations of the fate of the tyrant Tarquin in early Rome:[2] William
Bond's *The Tuscan Treaty; Or, Tarquin's Overthrow* at Covent
Garden, 1733; and William Duncombe's *Junius Brutus* at
Drury Lane, 1734. The former had only such political relevance
as was implicit in the portrayal of a tyrant's fall. Duncombe's
Junius Brutus, however, was a more pointed and specific commentary on the times. Based on Voltaire's *Brutus*, the tragedy
celebrates William III, represented by the title character (as
Duncombe acknowledges in his dedication); and it makes a
detailed defence of the constitutional principles inherent in the
Revolution of 1688. Tarquin's subversion of Roman law constituted an annullment of the senators' oath of allegiance to him,
Brutus explains in a patent allusion to English history (1):

He promis'd to maintain the Rights of *Rome*:
This was the Bond between the King and People.
Our Oaths are cancell'd by the Breach of His.

The central application intended by Duncombe is to the

---

[1] *Memoirs*, ed. Sedgwick, iii. 839: '. . . in that part of the play (which was *Cato*)
where Cato says these words—"when vice prevails, and impious men bear sway,
the post of honour is a private station"—there was another loud huzza, with a great
clap, in the latter part of which applause the Prince himself joined in the face of
the whole audience.'

[2] For Nathaniel Lee's earlier dramatization of this subject, see above, pp. 15-17.

Revolution, but certain passages clearly reflect on Walpole's Government.[1] Although Duncombe protested his innocence of such an intention, he could scarcely have been ingenuous in doing so. The opposition ring of the following boast of Brutus (1) is clear enough:

> We, and these Senators, Foes to Corruption,
> Have heap'd no Wealth, tho' hoary grown in Honours:
> Take then the Gold: Let *Tarquin* revel with it,
> Nor envy us our Poverty and Freedom.

Here is the opposition boast of a noble simplicity, of a contempt of luxury, a boast that by 1734 was so conventional in its application it could not be misunderstood.[2]

As we have seen, the clamour against Walpole frequently took the form of denunciation of the peace policy that he so resolutely pursued until virtually forced into war with Spain. From the time of the Treaty of Utrecht England's relations with Spain had been difficult; they had in fact led to hostilities in 1718 and again in 1727. In the earlier instance Walpole had not yet come to first place in the Government; in the later he participated in the negotiations that prevented the outbreak of general war. The Treaty of Seville in 1729 settled temporarily the most urgent issues in dispute, but not to the satisfaction of many, who charged Walpole with neglect of the national interest. *The Craftsman* protested in 1729 about the indignities to which English ships were submitted by the Spanish, and throughout the 1730's opposition writers chided the nation for failing to respond manfully to injuries against the national honour.[3] From 1737 the cries for war grew more strident, Pope and Samuel Johnson joining in with their strong voices in the following year,[4] and at length, in October 1739, Walpole gave way and the nation went to war amid national rejoicing.

Apart from chauvinism, a principal motive for undertaking the war was a desire to protect and enlarge English trade with the Americas, which had been restricted by the Spaniards in their own interest. Hence the English merchants were among the

---

[1] James J. Lynch, *Box, Pit, and Gallery: Stage and Society in Johnson's London* (Berkeley and Los Angeles, 1953), p. 248.

[2] Cf. McKillop, *Background of Thomson's 'Liberty'*, pp. 86–87.

[3] Mabel D. Hessler, 'The Literary Opposition to Sir Robert Walpole, 1721–1742' (unpublished dissertation, University of Chicago, 1934), p. 29.

[4] Ibid., p. 100.

strongest proponents of the war, a circumstance that helps to account for George Lillo's introducing into *The London Merchant; Or, The History of George Barnwell* (Drury Lane, 1731) a load of dramatically irrelevant denunciation of the Spaniards. Again in *The Christian Hero* and in *Fatal Curiosity* (Little Theatre in the Haymarket, 1736), Lillo sounds bellicose notes which his audience would have understood as incitements to war. In the former play, the propaganda has dramatic appropriateness, but in the latter it is as little relevant to the action as is that in *The London Merchant*. 'There's now no insolence that *Spain* can offer', says old Wilmot in *Fatal Curiosity* (i), referring ostensibly to the Elizabethan age in which the play is set,

> But to the shame of this pacifick reign,
> Poor *England* must submit to —

And everyone in the audience would have understood Lillo's meaning. Aaron Hill dramatized the 'black legend' of Spanish treatment of the Indians in *Alzira* (Lincoln's Inn Fields, 1736), an adaptation from Voltaire. With a locale in Lima, Peru, the play provides a critique of Spanish policy in America, with emphasis on cruelty practised in the name of religion. William Havard's *King Charles the First* includes passages in the printed play that attack Walpole for failure to take reprisals against Spain. 'What must that Monarch be,' says Cromwell (iii),

> who lets one Man
> Ingross the Offices of Place and Pow'r,
> Who with the purloin'd Money of the State
> Buys Popularity, and whose careless Eye
> Sees our fair Trade destroy'd by *Corsair* Force,
> And Pirate Violence.

And Francis Lynch in *The Independent Patriot*, despite his implied acknowledgement that members of the opposition have impure motives, criticizes Walpole's foreign policy (cf. i). The war propaganda goes on in the theatres after the Licensing Act, rising indeed in crescendo, until in the masque of *Alfred* (1740) it reaches perfection of utterance in James Thomson's 'Britannia Rules the Waves', the most famous lyric ever to be inspired by a commercial war.

Most of the dramatists of the 1730's, whether they were propagandists or not, followed neoclassical precept in choosing characters of elevated station as their protagonists. The kings and emperors and noble Romans to whom I have alluded have company enough of their peers in other plays. But among the tragic protagonists there is one famous humble character: George Barnwell, an apprentice to a merchant, whose presence in tragedy at this time may be associated with political controversy, with the Whig propagandists' assertion of the dignity of the merchant class. Although an opposition play, George Lillo's *The London Merchant; Or, The History of George Barnwell*, first produced at Drury Lane in June 1731 and gaining thereafter an established place in the repertory, was emphatically a Whig play: a dramatization of the distinctively Whig conception of the merchant. As such it was a corollary in tragedy to Steele's *The Conscious Lovers* in comedy. Both plays were studied experiments, recognized by their authors and contemporary audiences as such, in the adaptation of their respective genres to the social fact of the rise of the great merchants to high place; in both we may observe Whig social doctrine subverting traditional conceptions of characterization. The doctrine of decorum in characterization, as expounded by such theorists as Dryden, Rymer, and Dennis, rested on social judgements more compatible with Tory than with Whig thought. It could not long retain its vitality once the Whig social programme was generally accepted, as it came to be during the reign of George II. The Tory conception of the financial community, to which Swift had given forceful expression in *The Examiner*, was, by the time of *The London Merchant*, an anachronism, though it retained sufficient vitality to provoke Lillo into introducing in dramatic dialogue a load of social theory that is only partially relevant to his action.

The London Merchant was not the first English domestic tragedy, nor even the first in the eighteenth century. The anonymous author of *Arden of Feversham*, Heywood, Otway, Southerne, Rowe, and Hill, among others, had written tragedies that may be so described, and with some of them at least Lillo was familiar, as appears from his allusion to Otway, Southerne, and Rowe in the prologue of his play and from his subsequent adaptation of *Arden of Feversham*. Yet the author of an essay in

The Weekly Register, 21 August 1731[1] (and it is reasonable to assume that he was speaking for many of his contemporaries), thought *The London Merchant* to be a dramatic innovation. Lillo himself seems to have so regarded the play. 'Considering the Novelty of this Attempt,' he wrote in his dedicatory epistle, 'I thought it would be expected from me to say something in its Excuse.'

There was good reason for the insistence on the 'novelty'. The tragedy is after all one in which the protagonist is of humble station, an apprentice, not as in those of several of Lillo's predecessors a member of the lesser gentry. Further, the tragedy is one in which the standard of conduct, the standard of honour, against which the protagonist is measured is derived from a commercial rather than from an aristocratic society. George Barnwell's crimes—fornication, theft, and murder— are, to be sure, crimes by any standard and they are so judged in the play; yet the milieu in which they are committed conditions the interpretation of them. Barnwell first violates the trust that his master places in him by an act of commercial dishonesty; his conduct is subjected throughout the play to a comparison with that of Trueman, an embodiment of the virtuous apprentice; and his tragic course is run to the accompaniment of sustained praise of the merchant. The play opens on a note of opposition Whig propaganda, an allusion to Spanish hostility, and Barnwell's master promptly establishes, explicitly, the standard of mercantile integrity that Barnwell subsequently violates.

The play is clumsy and patently doctrinaire. It bears only too obviously the signs of its origins in the early eighteenth-century controversies between the landed and moneyed interests and between the Walpole and the opposition Whigs. Still, it represents in its calculated breach of neoclassical principles an important dramatic innovation; and it was effective with audiences through most of the century. Much of the reason for its success no doubt lay in the contrast which it provided with the frigidly declamatory tragedies, tightly controlled by formalistic precept, of the neoclassical tradition. Yet the neoclassical tragedies continued to appear. For all of its contemporary success

---

[1] Reprinted in Loftis (ed.), *Essays on the Theatre from Eighteenth-Century Periodicals*, pp. 33–34.

and for all of the significance it would seem to have when we look retrospectively at the history of drama, *The London Merchant* was not much imitated in England. Such influence as it had is to be traced rather more through continental than through English dramatists.[1] It is largely an isolated phenomenon, an inept yet curiously moving monument to Lillo's determination to assert the dignity of his class, which was then so vigorously championed by the Whigs.

[1] See Lawrence Marsden Price, 'George Barnwell Abroad', *Comparative Literature*, ii (1950), 126–56.

VI

FIELDING AND THE STAGE LICENSING
ACT OF 1737

THE Licensing Act seemed to contemporaries, as it has
seemed to historians, a measure supported by Walpole for
the partisan ends of curbing attacks on himself and his
Ministry. However valid, this traditional conception of the Act
is scarcely comprehensive. As will be clear from the preceding
chapters, whatever Walpole's motives may have been the Act
that he supported gave legal reality to the recommendations of
a long series of commentators on theatrical affairs; it is indeed
in a restricted sense the culmination of the stage controversy
initiated by Collier's *Short View* in 1698. Nearly all of those who
wrote seriously about the theatres in the early eighteenth
century wanted more, not less, governmental supervision;
and many of them wanted the kind of controls that the
Licensing Act brought: closer supervisory powers in the hands
of the Lord Chamberlain and a restriction of the number of
theatres.

The demands for effective governmental regulation began
before 1698 and continued until the Government in 1737 took
decisive action. But if there is continuity in the demands, there
are modifications in the grounds on which they were based. In
the years just after the publication of *A Short View* and throughout Queen Anne's reign, the clamour for regulation was provoked by the licentiousness of the stage; critics urged the
Government to take effective measures to improve its moral tone.
In the years of George I's reign, from 1714 to 1727, years that
coincide with the prominence of the actor-managers at Drury
Lane, the clamour was occasioned not so much by moralistic as
by artistic offences. Critics objected to the control of the stage
by 'mere actors', who, in devoting excessive attention to 'non-
rational' entertainments such as pantomimes and dances, discouraged promising dramatists from writing new plays. Then

finally in the years after George II's accession, and especially after the huge success of *The Beggar's Opera*, the clamour for regulation was raised in response to the use of drama as a vehicle for political propaganda.

Those who sought to maintain the existing conditions often argued that freedom of expression on the stage was an extension of freedom of the press, and that to limit the one was to endanger the other. Fielding, so influential in provoking the Licensing Act, implied as much in the dedicatory epistle of *The Historical Register*; yet he included in the play, in the episode of Quidam's (or Walpole's) fiddling for the dance of the patriots, remarks that might be considered libellous even within an enlightened theory. The lack of restraint evident in the satirical allusions to Walpole could scarcely be allowed to continue. We must remember that in the most liberal interpretation of freedom of the press (and thus by extension of dramatic expression), absolute freedom to say anything is not envisaged. A modern authority on the subject thus explains the matter:

> Government must necessarily exert some control over the press as it must over all other types of institutions operating in society. All agree that it is the function of government to protect private reputations, to control to some unspecified degree the distribution of obscene matter, and to regulate to a still more vague degree publications which undermine the basic structure of organized society. Henry VIII, John Milton, John Locke, Walpole, George III, and even Lord Erskine agree that some government control of the press is necessary. The principal disagreements arise over the standards to be applied in devising and administering controls designed to protect the third objective mentioned above, the preservation of the basic structure of organized society.[1]

The crucial distinctions are thus ones that require interpretation in specific instances, and the interpretation will carry an air of controversy. Certainly the interpretation as applied to the dramatic satire of the 1730's is intensely controversial. Yet in historical retrospect it is less surprising that the Government took action in 1737 to curb the dramatists than that it tolerated for so long such a large body of dramatic abuse directed pointedly and personally at the chief Ministers of State. The

---

[1] Frederick S. Siebert, *Freedom of the Press in England, 1476–1776* (Urbana, Ill., 1952), pp. 9–10.

Licensing Act had an inhibiting effect on the development of drama, and it is for that reason to be regretted; but it was legislation for which there was strong provocation.

With Gay's death and Cibber's retirement from the Drury Lane management, both in 1732, the stage had lost its two most controversial figures. But whatever loss ensued in political excitement was soon compensated for by the vigorous activities of Fielding. In political satire, as indeed in all aspects of drama in that decade, his plays represent a culmination of what other, less gifted persons attempted. His plays are like theirs in theme, tone, and subject, but are more subtle and vigorous, just as they certainly were more effective in castigating Walpole. His work may be seen as the climax of the dramatic era, leading swiftly to its catastrophe in the Licensing Act.

As we have seen, Fielding made mild excursions into political satire as early as March 1730 in the burlesque of Cibber in *The Author's Farce* and April 1730 in the burlesque of 'the great man' who is the title character of *Tom Thumb*, both produced at the Little Theatre in the Haymarket; and bolder excursions the following year in *The Welsh Opera*, a burlesque treatment of the quarrel between Walpole and Pulteney in which he glanced satirically at the royal family.[1] He was becoming over-bold, and when he rewrote *The Welsh Opera* as *The Grub-Street Opera* he met resistance for the first time. The play was prohibited and the Little Theatre itself was submitted to harassment.[2] Yet although Fielding had been bold enough in his burlesques, he had not thus far identified himself as an opposition dramatist, having satirized its leaders along with Walpole, and hence when difficulties came at the Little Theatre, he could migrate along with a number of actors to Drury Lane, which with Cibber at the end of his long reign had an association with the Court party.[3] Fielding then made an effort to secure Walpole's patronage, dedicating the published version of *The Modern Husband* to him after it was produced in the theatre early in 1732. It is not known whether Walpole made any acknowledgement of the dedication; certainly he did not make one sufficiently attractive to hold

[1] Brown, 'Henry Fielding's *Grub-Street Opera*', loc. cit.
[2] Cross, *Fielding*, i. 110–12.
[3] Ibid. 113–16.

Fielding's allegiance. Nevertheless, by the dedication Fielding made himself a target for *The Grub-Street Journal*.

It was prompt to attack, printing on 30 March 1732 a letter signed 'Dramaticus', which most thoroughly damned the play on moral and artistic grounds.[1] Fielding replied in the 'Prolegomena' published with his next play, *The Covent-Garden Tragedy*, first acted at Drury Lane on 1 June 1732; in this, 'A Criticism on the Covent-Garden Tragedy, originally intended for the Grub Street Journal', he burlesqued the dramatic criticism appearing in that journal. His remarks called forth a torrent of abuse, extending over a period of three months (June to September), the chief burden of which was that his plays were obscene. It would be an oversimplification to regard this outburst as motivated solely by political animus; *The Modern Husband*, in its portrayal of sordid aspects of high life in London, is vulnerable to criticism, and the writer of *The Grub-Street Journal* was no mere party lackey. Yet it is scarcely coincidence that this hostility coincided with Fielding's bid for Walpole's patronage. Again, it is probably more than coincidence that the journal grew more kindly in the later years of the decade when Fielding himself became Walpole's severe critic. His *Pasquin* of 1736, it is true, drew criticism from the journal, but no sustained vituperation of the kind that had greeted his earlier plays.[2]

After *The Modern Husband*, Fielding made no more overtures to Walpole for support. Even so, he could scarcely associate himself with the opposition so long as his plays were produced at Drury Lane, as they were until early in 1734.[3] Hence, when in

---

[1] Hillhouse, *Grub-Street Journal*, p. 173. Fielding was supported against *The Grub-Street Journal* in 1732 by his friend Thomas Cooke, who in the June issue of his monthly *The Comedian, or Philosophical Enquirer* (No. 3) answered the criticism of *The Modern Husband*. Fielding himself replied in a letter (signed 'Philalethes') printed in *The Daily Post*, 31 July 1732, which is largely given over to rebuttal of *The Grub-Street Journal*'s charge of obscenity directed at *The Covent-Garden Tragedy*. *The Daily Post*, in which Fielding's letter appeared, had included the month before a puff for his *The Mock Doctor* (Drury Lane, June 1732) as well as a preliminary answer, in the form of a pseudonymous letter, to *The Grub-Street Journal*'s attack on him. This letter was also printed in *The London Evening Post*. These two newspapers, even though sympathetic to Fielding, both appear to have had an opposition bias (though the allegiance of *The Daily Post* is not certain). For the moment there was at least a partial incongruity between political and theatrical preferences.

[2] Hillhouse, *Grub-Street Journal*, pp. 182–3.

[3] He seems nevertheless to have made passing allusion to Walpole in his plays—

the spring of that year he made his first unmistakable overture to Walpole's enemies, he presented his play, *Don Quixote in England*, at the Little Theatre in the Haymarket. It is his dedication to the published play rather than anything in the play itself that reveals his political inclination, a dedication addressed to the Earl of Chesterfield (who had recently lost his place at Court by failure to follow Walpole's lead in the dispute on the Excise Bill) as a person 'who hath so gloriously distinguished Himself in the Cause of Liberty'. Fielding associated his comedy with the same cause. 'I fansy a lively Representation of the Calamities brought on a Country by general Corruption, might have a very sensible and useful Effect on the Spectators', he wrote, in what certainly was intended and must have been understood by Chesterfield and his fellow leaders in opposition as a bid for patronage—one that was not to be accepted with any enthusiasm until two years later. The play, with a locale at '*An Inn in a Country Borough*', depicts an election, its focus on the stratagems adopted by opposing Parliamentary candidates to win votes. Don Quixote, himself a candidate, provides in his naïve incomprehension of the schemings of those surrounding him a dramatic vehicle for emphasizing the wholesale corruption. The country electors, in their eagerness to be bribed, are as much butts of Fielding's satire as the candidates for office, whose party affiliations are not clearly established. There is in fact an impartiality in the satire, an absence of partisanship for Court or Country, as well as a genial gusto in the depiction of the characters and institutions of rural England, which contributes to the attractiveness of the play even while it diminishes its propagandistic force.

Fielding's next major essay into political satire, *Pasquin* (March 1736), was bolder, more bitter, more openly partisan, and much more successful. This time he was the leader of a theatrical company and could produce his own play, and this time the opposition recognized him as one of their own.[1] Having had the play rejected by Rich at Covent Garden and perhaps by Fleetwood at Drury Lane, Fielding turned to the Little Theatre in the Haymarket and himself reorganized a group of young

as in *The Mock Doctor*, Drury Lane 1732 (Baker, 'Political Allusion in Fielding', loc. cit.).

[1] Cross, *Fielding*, i. 177–91.

actors who had appeared there for several seasons into 'The Great Mogul's Company of Comedians', the facetious title suggesting the absolute power of a stage manager to decide the fate of aspiring dramatists.[1] Like *The Author's Farce* (1730), *Pasquin* is ostensibly a stage rehearsal; it has thematic as well as structural similarities to the earlier play, though it differs in that it presents not one stage rehearsal but two, of a comedy and a tragedy, both hostile to Walpole. The hits in the comedy are the more obvious, and they were recognized from the beginning, whereas those in the tragedy were understood only after some time had passed.[2] Called *The Election*, the comedy is yet another treatment of the stratagems by which seats in Parliament were bought or sought after with money. The fiction of the rehearsal is satirically useful in that the supposed spectators are enabled to make interpretive remarks—as when the author, Trapwit, instructs an actor playing the part of a man standing for Parliament to 'Bribe a little more openly . . . or the Audience will lose that Joke'. Fielding depicts the deliberations of the mayor and aldermen of a town as they try to decide between rival candidates, two of the Country party and the other two of the Court interest; and although they make what he regards as the right choice and elect the Country candidates (their own neighbours), the mayor under pressure from his wife declares the Court candidates elected. If unmistakably partisan this time, Fielding nevertheless makes a dramatic acknowledgement, as he had earlier in *Don Quixote*, that the Court party has no monopoly on corruption.

In the parallel rehearsal of the tragedy, Fielding plays variations on the dunciad theme, which had been popular in the eighteenth century even before Pope brought it to high artistic statement in the first version of his poem. Fustian's tragedy in *Pasquin* owes something to the earlier versions of *The Dunciad*, and Pope in turn apparently took suggestions from it for the later fourth book of *The Dunciad*. Fielding portrays the contention of Queen Ignorance and Queen Common-Sense; and in allotting victory to the former, he implies a comprehensive judgement on the culture of England. He thus conveys criticism of Walpole in his central allegory, representing the extension of

---

[1] Ibid. 178.
[2] Ibid. 189–90.

the realm of Ignorance over that of Common-Sense. The specific allusions to Walpole and his policies, of which there are several, merely give emphasis to the comprehensive damnation that is the theme of the whole.[1] 'Why should a wise Man wish to think', asks Queen Ignorance, and frustrated Patriots would have understood her (v),

> when Thought
> Still hurts his Pride? In spite of all his Art,
> Malicious Fortune, by a lucky Train
> Of Accidents, shall still defeat his Schemes,
> And set the greatest Blunderer above him.

After fifteen years of Walpole's supremacy, years during which (in the opposition view) men of literary and intellectual distinction had been systematically discouraged, this would have been roundly applauded by the audiences that crowded to the Little Theatre in the Haymarket.[2]

Pasquin was in fact a success of the proportions of *The Beggar's Opera*. For more than sixty nights it drew audiences that included the brilliant and fashionable. Fielding was rewarded with the friendship of George Lyttelton, William Pitt, the Earl of Chesterfield, and the Duke of Bedford.[3] When Chesterfield and Lyttelton in February 1737 founded a new journal as a supplement to *The Craftsman*, they called it *Common Sense*, as a compliment to Fielding and in acknowledgement of their shared objectives. Yet Fielding's very success proved to be a hazard, for it made him bolder at the same time that it gave the alarm to Walpole and made him more cautious.[4]

When in March 1737 Fielding brought out *The Historical Register*, he was more openly hostile to Walpole than he had been before, less inclined to satirize corruption impartially. Here again he depends on a blend of theatrical and political satire. In his 'Dedication to the Public' prefixed to the published version he reviews the threats to the 'constitution of the British theatre'

[1] George Sherburn, '*The Dunciad*, Book IV', in *Studies in English, Department of English, the University of Texas* (Austin, Tex., 1945), pp. 174–90; Hessler, 'Literary Opposition to Walpole', pp. 133–4.

[2] Fielding's burlesque of John Rich's pantomimes, *Tumble-Down Dick*, presented at the Haymarket that same spring, includes further hits at Walpole (Baker, 'Political Allusion in Fielding', loc. cit.).

[3] Cross, *Fielding*, i. 179.

[4] Emmett L. Avery, 'Fielding's Last Season with the Haymarket Theatre', *Modern Philology*, xxxvi (1939), 283–92.

in current managerial practices, and in doing so catalogues the customary charges against Walpole; in characterizing Pistol in the play itself he exploits the long-established association of theatre manager and Prime Minister. (Pistol was a generally accepted name for Theophilus Cibber; the fact that his father, as manager of Drury Lane, had been used by opposition journalists to symbolize Walpole the Prime Minister gave special point to the theatre-government metaphor.) Fielding explains in his dedication with a bluntness he had previously avoided who was represented by the character Quidam:

> Who is this *Quidam?* . . . Who but the Devil could act such a Part? . . . Indeed it is so plain who is meant by this *Quidam*, that he who maketh any wrong Application thereof might as well mistake the Name of *Thomas* for *John* [an allusion apparently to the Duke of Newcastle and Lord Hervey], or old *Nick* for old *Bob*.

And at the end of the play when Quidam gives money to a group of patriots, who as Mr. Medley explains have holes in their pockets, and then fiddles while they dance off the stage, leaving the money behind—in this episode Fielding depicts Walpole's bribery of his opponents, such persons as Lord Hervey, whom he had already brought over, and perhaps also those members of the opposition who then followed Pulteney and Carteret, suspected by Chesterfield and Lyttelton of being vulnerable to bribery.[1]

To some of the performances of *The Historical Register* that spring Fielding added an afterpiece, a burlesque tragedy entitled *Eurydice Hissed; Or, a Word to the Wise*, which cleverly extended the satirical identification of the theatrical and political worlds.[2] Loosely autobiographical, portraying Fielding's progress from success in *Pasquin* to failure in the farce *Eurydice* (which he had presented earlier in the same year at Drury Lane), the burlesque is at the same time an allegory of Walpole's progress from success with Parliament to failure in the Excise Bill. The contemporary reaction to the play may be inferred from an entry in the diary of the Earl of Egmont, who saw it on 18 April 1737:

> I dined at home, and then went to the Haymarket Playhouse, where a farce was acted called *Eurydice First* [apparently an error for

[1] Hessler, 'Literary Opposition to Walpole', pp. 138–9.
[2] Charles B. Woods, 'Notes on Three of Fielding's Plays', *PMLA*, lii (1937), 368–73.

Eurydice Hissed], an allegory on the loss of the Excise Bill. The whole was a satire on Sir Robert Walpole, and I observed that when any strong passages fell, the Prince, who was there, clapped, especially when in favour of liberty.[1]

The very name of the chief character, Pillage, would have suggested Walpole; and Pillage's experience with a hostile 'House' (Commons as well as the theatrical audience) parallels Walpole's experience with the 'farce' of the Excise Bill.

In its final season 'Mr. Fielding's Scandal Shop', as the Little Theatre in the Haymarket came to be known, was thus a focus of boisterous opposition gaiety.[2] As noted by Lord Egmont, the Prince of Wales attended, emphasizing with his applause the political hits. We may be sure that there was more political innuendo at the theatre than that of which record remains.[3] Fielding presented a farce in January called *The Fall of Bob, alias Gin* (which apparently was not printed); and he revived *Pasquin* in February for a single performance, presenting it again in the spring. Toward the close of the season, apparently not anticipating the parliamentary action against the stage, he advertised two pieces which may be assumed by their titles to have been political:

Never acted before. By the Great Mogul's Company of Comedians. . . . will be presented MACHEATH turn'd PYRATE: or, POLLY in INDIA. An Opera. Very much taken, if not improv'd from the famous Sequel of the late celebrated Mr. Gay, with a new Prologue proper to the Occasion. And after the Run of that, the Town will be entertain'd with a new Farce of two Acts, call'd The KING and TITI: or, The MEDLARS. Taken from the History of King Titi. Originally written in French, and lately translated into English.[4]

The implications of such a title as *Polly in India* require no explanation; those of *The King and Titi* would have been evident in 1737. The previous year a French work had appeared in Paris with the title *Histoire du Prince Titi, A.B.* and had been promptly translated into English and published in London, where it was interpreted as a complimentary portrait of the Prince of Wales and an uncomplimentary one of his parents.

[1] Quoted from Woods, *PLMA*, lii (1937), p. 369.

[2] Cf. Laprade, *Public Opinion and Politics*, p. 383.

[3] See Avery, 'Fielding's Last Season with the Haymarket Theatre', loc. cit.

[4] *Daily Advertiser*, 25 May 1737. A performance of *Polly in India* was announced for 30 May (Avery, 'Fielding's Last Season with the Haymarket Theatre', p. 290).

Knowing the literary strategy of the opposition in these years, we may guess what Fielding and his associates had in mind.

With such intensely partisan plays as *Pasquin* and *The Historical Register* Fielding understandably drew comment that, in part at least, followed party lines.[1] The journalistic debate over the burlesques, which led to debate over the Bill for licensing the stage, began in earnest when *The Daily Gazetteer*, Walpole's principal organ, was moved by *The Historical Register* and its afterpiece, *Eurydice Hissed*, to print an open letter on 7 May 1737 warning that there was danger ahead if Fielding persisted with his satires.[2] This letter, which may have been written by a person of high rank,[3] proved to be the first of a series that appeared in *The Daily Gazetteer*, containing informed and well-reasoned arguments for governmental regulation of the stage. A portion of the letter merits quotation:

> The ELECTION, (a *Comedy in Pasquin*) laid the Foundation for introducing POLITICKS on the Stage; but as the Author was general in his Satyr, and exposed with Wit and Humour, the Practices of *Elections*, without coming so near, as to point *any Person* out, he was not then guilty of the Fault he has since committed; tho' I cannot think him *Praiseworthy*, for turning into Ridicule and making slight of one of the *gravest* Evils our Constitution is subject to: 'Twas as ill judged, as the late Mr. *Gay's* turning *Highwaymen*, *Pickpockets*, and *Whores* into *Heroes* and *Heroines*, which (tho' done with all the Wit and Humour conceivable in Man) served only to increase the Number of those *corrupt* Wretches who encouraged one another, from the Example of the Stage, which exposed with *Wit*, what ought to be punished with *Rigour*.

Fielding was prompt in his own defence, addressing in reply a letter 'To the Author of Common Sense', in which journal it was printed on 21 May 1737. His tone is flippant and he echoes opposition commonplaces, but he nevertheless attempts reasoned rebuttal. Among other arguments he insists, as he was altogether justified in doing, that *Pasquin* was not 'the first Introducer of

---

[1] *The Grub-Street Journal* printed severe criticism of *Pasquin* (in Nos. 330 and 332, April and May 1736), but not prolonged denigration of Fielding in any way approximating that with which it greeted his plays when he was nominally in Walpole's camp, and in fact praised his satire on corruption in politics.
[2] The letter is reprinted in Loftis (ed.), *Essays on the Theatre from Eighteenth-Century Periodicals*, pp. 54–57.
[3] Perhaps Lord Hervey. Cf. Cross, *Fielding*, i. 219.

Things of this Kind'. A further letter appeared in *The Daily Gazetteer*, 4 June 1737, the writer this time using the historical argument that the Greeks had been led to supervision of the stage by Aristophanes' introduction of public figures into plays; and he significantly links Fielding with the proposed Parliamentary action: 'I BELIEVE, and am confident, the Government had no Thought of vesting any Power in any Great *Officers* Hands for this Purpose, had not you *pav'd* the Way for the Subversion of the Stage, by introducing on it Matters quite foreign to its true Object.' Associating political satire with offences against morality, he observes that *The Beggar's Opera* is calculated to reduce the horror and aversion the spectator feels for criminals. The debate continued, *The Craftsman* taking up the case for the opposition and *The Daily Gazetteer* carrying on for the Ministry. Amid the quarreling there is some illumination of problems inherent in governmental supervision of the stage. Meanwhile, the Licensing Bill passed through Parliament and received, on 21 June 1737, the Royal Assent.

In order to assess eighteenth-century attitudes toward governmental responsibility for the stage, we must distinguish between two different areas of that responsibility: for theatrical companies on the one hand, and for dramatists on the other.[1] The distinction is important and was frequently made by contemporaries; it is illuminated by attitudes expressed two years earlier toward a Bill for the closer regulation of the stage that Parliament considered but did not pass. Supported by, among others, Sir John Barnard, a representative in Commons of the City of London, the Bill 'for restraining the Number of Houses for playing of Interludes' was read for the first time in April 1735.[2] It would, in brief, have prohibited all theatrical companies except those which operated by the authority of royal patents. Barnard's support of the Bill and the tenor of the petitions submitted to Parliament about it suggest that its backers were moved by a desire to curb theatrical companies, not to limit dramatic authors in satirical attacks on the Govern-

---

[1] The distinction is explained by Victor, *History of the Theatres*, i. 49–50.

[2] P. J. Crean, 'The Stage Licensing Act of 1737', *Modern Philology*, xxxv (1937–8), 243. See Crean and also Scouten, *London Stage*, i. xlviii–lx, for detailed accounts of the Licensing Act.

ment.[1] In particular, Barnard and other leading citizens were troubled by the continued existence of Goodman's Fields, which, in the City proper, allegedly encouraged vice and debauchery.

Many petitions and personal appeals against the Bill were directed to Parliament,[2] but its failure seems to have been due to an amendment introduced by Walpole that led to its entanglement in the controversy between Ministry and opposition. Walpole proposed to confirm the Lord Chamberlain's authority in theatrical affairs, including the authority to supervise (i.e. censor) the plays presented. Coxe, Walpole's eighteenth-century biographer, explains that it was 'insinuated' in the House of Commons that the King would not sign the Bill unless this addition was made to it, whereupon Barnard, recalling what he considered wanton abuses of the Lord Chamberlain's power (including the prohibition of *Polly*), decided to withdraw the Bill, rather than to convey to a Court officer power that could be used arbitrarily.[3] We may guess the motives that led Barnard to his action. Himself one of the leaders in the successful fight against the Excise scheme of 1733, he would have felt too much sympathy for Walpole's critics to desire passage of legislation designed to shield him from the attacks of dramatic satirists. The provision in the Bill for censorship, that is to say, made it unacceptable to Barnard and others who had supported it as a means to reducing the number of theatres and reviving a closer supervision of the internal affairs of those permitted to operate. Control over the theatres themselves was one thing; control over the dramatists another.

Fielding in 1736 and 1737, as we have seen, made dramatic satire such a forceful political weapon that Walpole was compelled to give it his attention. Still, it was not Fielding (or at

---

[1] The petitions are described in Percy Fitzgerald, *A New History of the English Stage* (London, 1882), ii. 101–3.

[2] Including an informative one from a group of actors: 'The Case of James Mills, Benjamin Johnson, James Quin . . . [and others] in Behalf of themselves and the Rest of the Comedians of the Theatres-Royal of Drury-Lane and Covent-Garden.' (Copy in the Huntington Library.)

[3] William Coxe, *Memoirs of the Life and Administration of Sir Robert Walpole, Earl of Orford* (London, 1798), i. 515. In Richard Chandler, *The History and Proceedings of the House of Commons* (London, 1742, &c.), ix. 94, it is asserted that the Bill failed 'on Account of a Clause offer'd to be inserted in the said Bill for enlarging the Power of the Lord Chamberlain with regard to the Licensing of Plays'. (Quoted from Crean, op. cit., p. 248 n.)

least probably not) but someone else who provided the pretext for the Licensing Act. This unidentified person wrote a scurrilous play that has not survived, a dramatization of a satire entitled *The Vision of the Golden Rump*, which in its original form was published in March 1737 in *Common Sense*. We may merely guess at the nature of the play from such descriptions of it as have survived and from the satire on which it was based. 'The Vision' of the title seems to have been one of an Indian religious ceremony in which a person identifiable with Walpole led his fellow worshippers in adoration of gigantic golden buttocks. It was so lewd and so direct in allusion to Walpole and even to the King that it served Walpole as an exhibit by which he could demonstrate the need for regulatory legislation.

The very usefulness to Walpole of this outrageous play raises questions concerning its origin. Walpole obtained a manuscript copy of it from Henry Giffard, formerly at Goodman's Fields, but then at Lincoln's Inn Fields; where Giffard acquired it or what his motives were in turning it over to Walpole we do not know. Walpole kept it, paid Giffard for it, read excerpts from it in the House of Commons—and accomplished his purpose. Indeed, so useful was the play to him that there is at least the possibility that it was written at his instigation. This at any rate is the view advanced several years later in a burlesque autobiography of Theophilus Cibber, the anonymous *An Apology for the Life of Mr. T. . . . . C . . . . . ., Comedian* (1740):

Mr. *Giffard* had remov'd about this Time from *Goodman's Fields* to *Lincoln's Inn Fields* House, which he had hir'd of Mr. *Rich*: His Removal had not answer'd his End, and his Affairs began to grow desperate. He had never as yet given any prejudicial Offence to the Court, yet was suppos'd not to have such Obligations to it, as to deny, at this Juncture, the performing a Farce which might bring him a large Sum of Money. At this same Time, in a most vile Paper, call'd *Common Sense*, there was a libellous Production call'd the *Golden Rump*, which the Town and the Mob were Fools enough to think Wit and Humour: Now as the hitting in with the Humour of the multitudinous Mob is very advantageous to a Theatre, a Dramatick Piece was wrote on this *Golden Rump* Subject, and call'd the *Golden Rump*, which was given Mr. *Giffard* to be perform'd; but before it was rehears'd it so happen'd, no Matter how or why, but so it happen'd, that Mr. *Giffard* went to *Downing-Street* with this Satirical Farce in his Pocket, which was delivered to a *great Man* for his

Perusal; and it was found to be a scurrilous, ignominious . . . Libel
against Majesty itself. It was immediately carried to, — shown to, —
explain'd to, — and remonstrated to, — that if there was not an
immediate Act of Parliament to stop such Abuses, not Regal Dignity
was safe from them. . . . The Point gain'd in a Moment, and a proper
Act order'd to be got. . . . Suppose, Sir, this same *Golden Rump* Farce
was wrote by a certain great Man's own Direction, and as much
Scurrility and Treason larded in it as possible. — Suppose *Giffard*
had a private Hint how to act in this Affair, and was promis'd great
Things to play a particular Part in this Farce. — Suppose he was
promis'd a *separate Licence*, or an Equivalent: — You may then
suppose the M. . . . a thorough Politician, who knew to manage bad
Things to the best Advantage. . . . If you are so ungenteel to require
Proof demonstrative I have done with you, and can only refer you
to the Author and Negociators of the *Golden Rump*. — This, however,
is notoriously certain, that the Farce of the *Golden Rump* was carried
to a great Man, and the Master of the Playhouse, who carried it,
was promised something, which he has been some Time in a vain
Expectation of, but will now, in all Probability, end in nothing at
all.[1]

This account is unconfirmed, as the author acknowledges. It is
not implausible; it fits the known facts—but more we cannot say.

It seems at any rate more plausible than the opinion expressed by Horace Walpole that the play was written by Fielding. Horace Walpole, who found an imperfect copy of it among
his father's papers after his death, says flatly (but without
giving his source of information) that Fielding wrote it; and
that Walpole 'got the piece into his hands . . . and then procured
the act to be passed for regulating the stage'.[2] He does not allude
to Giffard, who certainly had a part in the affair; and he says
that the play was intended for performance at the Little Theatre
in the Haymarket, where Fielding's company then acted. But
would Fielding have written such a coarsely vulgar piece? If so,
would he not have been prosecuted for libel? And how came
Henry Giffard to get a copy of it? The statement of a person
with such special sources of information as Horace Walpole
must be considered; but there nevertheless seem to be too many
difficulties for us to accept it.

---

[1] Pp. 93–94. Fielding may have contributed to this burlesque autobiography
(cf. Cross, *Fielding*, iii. 337).

[2] *Memoirs of the Reign of King George the Second*, ed. Lord Holland, second edition
(London, 1847), i. 13–14 n.

The Licensing Bill passed easily through both Houses of Parliament in May and June, and, as already noted, on 21 June it received the Royal Assent to become law. In form it was merely an amendment to a piece of earlier legislation, the vagrancy act of the twelfth year of Queen Anne. Walpole presumably employed the form of an amendment for reasons of strategy, to avoid conveying the impression that anything radically new was contemplated. Whatever his motive there was a certain propriety in the form, for the Licensing Act introduced little if anything for which there was not precedent in the previous half-century. The Act had two major provisions: it prohibited all theatres except those which held royal patents or were licensed by the Lord Chamberlain; and it required that thenceforth copies of all new plays, additions to old plays, and prologues and epilogues should be submitted to the Lord Chamberlain for licensing at least two weeks before performance.[1] The latter of the two provisions evoked the more eloquent protests, but the former, I think, had the more inhibiting effect on the development of drama.

So thoroughly was the debate over the Licensing Act assimilated into the controversy between Walpole and his enemies that considerations of principles of theatre government were obscured or distorted. To the opposition the Act represented a notable instance of Walpole's infringement of English liberties, further evidence in support of their charge that he had despotic powers in view. They had the preponderance of literary talent on their side; the memorable statements evoked by the Act, Lord Chesterfield's and Samuel Johnson's, made their opinions articulate. Yet if effective in the controversy, these statements in large measure fall wide of the mark, eloquently making points that were not in dispute and ignoring others that emphatically were.

As we have seen, the principle of governmental control of the theatres themselves was generally accepted. Consequently, the opposition spokesmen focused on the provisions for licensing plays and ignored or almost ignored the provisions for limiting

---

[1] The Act further prohibited theatrical performances 'except in the City of Westminster . . . and in such places where His Majesty, His Heirs and Successors shall in their Royal Persons reside, and during such Residence only . . . '.

the number of theatres. Their strategy turned on the association of freedom of expression on the stage with that of the press and hence with the liberty of publicly criticizing political leaders. Fielding on the eve of the Licensing Act had linked the two forms of freedom in his dedication of *The Historical Register*; Lord Chesterfield, in his speech against the Bill, professed to see it as a preliminary to a revival of licensing the press; James Thomson in the preface to a new edition of Milton's *Areopagitica* (January 1738) denounced censorship of the press with a vehemence that would seem to arise from the present fact of stage licensing;[1] Johnson included in his *Vindication of the Licensers of the Stage* an ironical 'plea' for the extension of 'the power of the licenser to the press'.[2] With the premise of opposition writers, that liberty of expression is desirable and the suppression of it dangerous, we may all agree; but we may wish that they had devoted more of their energies to analysing the principles of stage government and less to exhortations to the love of liberty.

Chesterfield's and Johnson's attacks on the Act merit special attention. They resemble one another in their common debt to the propagandistic tradition of the opposition, which encouraged an oversimplification of the differences separating Walpole from his critics; but they are unlike in their literary strategy. Chesterfield's speech purports to be an inclusive and closely reasoned demonstration; Johnson's tract is an ironical satire with a Swiftian tone of mock reasonableness. Johnson's work is the more entertaining; Chesterfield's the more enlightening.

Why the haste with which passage of the Bill is urged, Chesterfield asks; why should it be introduced so late in the season as to preclude careful consideration of it? He has heard, he says, alluding to the farce of *The Golden Rump*, of the pretended reason for haste; but this can be no sound reason. 'The dutiful behaviour of the players, the prudent caution they shewed upon that occasion, can never be a reason for subjecting them to such an arbitrary restraint. . . .'[3] Rather, the episode would suggest the adequacy of existing laws. He acknowledges

---

[1] Douglas Grant, *James Thomson: Poet of 'The Seasons'* (London, 1951), p. 177.
[2] *Works* (ed. Sir John Hawkins, London, 1787–1788), xiv. 55.
[3] *Works* (ed. M. Maty, London, 1777), vol. i, Part ii, 230.

and regrets the recent licentiousness of the stage; but this he attributes to the officers responsible having failed to prosecute rather than to a lack of adequate legislation. He alludes to two recent plays which although offensive were not the occasions for prosecution—referring certainly to Fielding's *Pasquin* and probably to William Havard's *King Charles the First*, a tragedy with 'a catastrophe too recent, too melancholy, and of too solemn a nature, to be heard of any where but from the pulpit'.[1] Citing examples from classical antiquity and from seventeenth-century France, he argues that dramatic satire can support public morality by criticizing faults even in individuals of high station otherwise largely immune from criticism. And he undertakes to show how the licensing of the stage must lead to that of the press and hence to the destruction of British liberty: 'It is an arrow, that does but glance upon the stage; the mortal wound seems designed against the liberty of the press.'[2]

Chesterfield's argument includes both opposition hyperbole and acute observation. After his extravagant prediction of the extinction of liberty, he considers the implications of granting increased authority to the Lord Chamberlain, isolating in so doing a distinctive quality of the Bill—that it would subject dramatists and actors to restraint before the commission of an offence rather than after. He urges that dramatists and actors be punished, like other persons, only after they have offended; that they be not subjected to the arbitrary power of the Chamberlain. A forceful argument—though it ignores the historical fact that Chamberlains long exercised just such arbitrary power and only recently had intermittently yielded it.

On the subject of politics in drama he employs a paradox: 'I shall admit, my lords, that the stage ought not, upon any occasion, to meddle with politics, but for that very reason among the rest, I am against the bill now before us.'[3] It would subject the stage so completely to the Court, he argues, that drama would perforce reflect Court politics. And here he cites tellingly the experience of the Restoration, when the stage was partisan to such an extent that Royalist attitude determined characterizations and the choice of dramatic subjects. The Bill, in his view, would inhibit dramatists from the satirical review of

---

[1] *Works* (ed. M. Maty, London, 1777). vol. 1, Part ii, 230–1.
[2] Ibid., p. 235.   [3] Ibid., p. 237.

Court follies and make them instead a medium for transmitting those follies to the rest of the nation.

Chesterfield's speech was much praised at the time he delivered it (though it did not prevent the Lords from passing the Bill), and it has been much praised since. It is an eloquent defence of freedom of expression. But its strength as a permanently valid defence of the freedom of the stage is a corollary of its limitations as an indictment of the Licensing Act, for it fails to acknowledge the ambiguity and confusion in the laws and traditions by which the stage had been regulated for the previous decade. That is to say, Chesterfield's arguments are effective as generalizations, but they lack the particularity to make them very useful in assessing the theatrical situation of the 1730's.

Both this merit and this liability are present in intensified form in Johnson's *A Complete Vindication of the Licensers of the Stage, from the Malicious and Scandalous Aspersions of Mr. Brooke, Author of 'Gustavus Vasa'*. The circumstances that prompted the two protests were quite different: Chesterfield spoke in the House of Lords just before the Bill passed; Johnson wrote two years later, when the Licenser first prohibited a play, Henry Brooke's *Gustavus Vasa*. Johnson had no need for the appearance of reasonable demonstration, but could employ an irony as Swiftian as he could make it. In an impassioned defence of freedom of the stage and an expression of hatred for despotism, even when practised by the petty tyrant which he believed the Licenser to be, Johnson echoes the opposition celebration of personal liberty. Altogether, in his Whiggish defence of individual freedom, he expresses opinions incongruous with the modern preconception of his political ideas.[1]

The mask or fictional identity that Johnson ironically assumes is one of a pamphleteer in the employ of Walpole, engaged to answer his critics. As naïvely imperceptive as Swift's spokesmen, the pamphleteer is unable to understand the motives that impel the Patriots to continue attacking the Court party, after a hundred defeats, when they can expect no reward except the approbation of posterity. The Romans were infected with a similar madness, which lasted until the destruction of Carthage, after which it declined and was, in a few years, extinguished.

[1] Cf. D. J. Greene, *The Politics of Samuel Johnson* (New Haven, 1960), pp. 99–105.

Recent poets, including Brooke, have been notoriously infected with a disease of the mind:

This temper . . . is almost always complicated with ideas of the high prerogatives of human nature, of a sacred unalienable birthright, which no man has conferred upon us, and which neither Kings can take, nor Senates give away; which we may justly assert whenever and by whomsoever it is attacked, and which, if ever it should happen to be lost, we may take the first opportunity to recover.[1]

Such ideas led Brooke to think that he deserved a licence for his play and occasioned his complaints when he did not receive one; they even led him to protest when the Licenser kept his play three weeks instead of the prescribed two. Brooke has failed to grasp the prime intention of the Licensing Act, 'which was only to bring poets into subjection and dependence, not to encourage good writers, but to discourage all'.[2] He has complained that his play was rejected without a reason assigned. But why, Johnson asks ironically, was the statute passed if not to permit the Licenser 'to do that *without* reason, which *with* reason he could do before'.[3] The jaunty phrase should not obscure the fact that Johnson renders an opinion on an important issue: he implies that the Licensing Act did not merely regularize an authority which the Lord Chamberlain had had all along, but conveyed to him new and arbitrary powers.

Johnson's allusions to and quotations from Brooke's play would be enough to indicate that the play follows the familiar pattern of opposition propaganda, even if we were unable to read it. Explicating key passages, the fictional pamphleteer expresses aversion to commonplaces of libertarian doctrine. His sensitivity to dramatic innuendo is such that he suggests, in a vein which *The Craftsman* had anticipated ten years before (No. 140, 8 March 1729), that an 'index expurgatorius' to old plays be prepared. Gaps in texts thus created could be filled by the Poet Laureate (Cibber). He urges licensing the press; and in a heavy-handed passage perhaps suggested by Swift's *Argument Against Abolishing Christianity*, he also urges the suppression of schools where reading is taught. If it should 'be made felony to teach to read without a license from the Lord Chamberlain',

---

[1] *Works,* xiv. 42.   [2] Ibid. 45.   [3] Ibid. 46.

then the licenser 'will in time enjoy the title and the salary without the trouble of exercising his power, and the nation will rest at length in ignorance and peace'.[1] We hear an echo of *The Dunciad*.

All of this is forceful and amusing if occasionally lacking in finesse; like Chesterfield's speech the tract will endure as a valid plea for freedom of expression from bureaucratic tyranny. But it is even less able than the speech to bear close scrutiny with reference to the occasion that prompted it. Johnson was factually wrong on almost every important point: the motives of the opposition were not disinterested; despite his implication to the contrary, Lord Chamberlains had acted arbitrarily before the Licensing Act; Henry Brooke's play was a political allegory, and it could reasonably be considered seditious; the Licensing Act was not a harbinger of licensing of the press. Even the phase of Roman history which he invoked was largely a myth. Johnson, in brief, felt no more obligation to circumstantial accuracy than opposition writers customarily did in the 1730's or in fact than have satirists in any era.

As I have said, the Licensing Act evoked no talent in its defence comparable to that of Chesterfield and Johnson. The most systematic statement of the Government's position resides in the letters printed in *The Daily Gazetteer* (May and June 1737), which I have already described. The Act itself was defended by Colley Cibber, whose discussions of it in his *Apology* (written in 1738) may be read in the context of the contemporary debate. Like almost everyone else who discussed the subject, he had private motives for the position he took. For years he had served opposition writers as a symbol for the kind of talent encouraged by Walpole; and he had suffered in particular from Fielding, who had introduced caricatures of him into his burlesques.[2] His defence of the Licensing Act was thus at once a defence of his patron and friend and an attack on his enemy. He was biased— but he nevertheless brought to the subject a firmer grasp of theatrical history than did anyone else who entered the controversy.

Unlike Chesterfield and Johnson, Cibber considers at length

---

[1] Ibid. 58.

[2] Houghton W. Taylor, 'Fielding upon Cibber', *Modern Philology*, xxix (1931), 73–90.

both of the important provisions of the Act, the control over the number of theatres as well as the licensing of plays. Reviewing the disputes of the previous decade that arose from uncertainty whether or not a company of actors required a licence in order to act, he alludes to the unsuccessful attempts to silence Goodman's Fields and discusses at length the patentees' efforts in 1733 to suppress the Little Theatre in the Haymarket.[1] On this occasion the patentees had invoked the same Act that as amended in 1737 became the Licensing Act, and John Harper, a player from the Haymarket, was in fact briefly imprisoned; but after a hearing in Westminster Hall he had been released. Cibber explains the implications of all this:

> The Issue of this Trial threw me at that time into a very odd Reflexion, *viz*. That if acting Plays without License did not make the Performers Vagabonds unless they wandered from their Habitations so to do, how particular was the Case of Us three late Menaging Actors at the *Theatre-Royal*, who in twenty Years before had paid upon an Averidge at least Twenty Thousand Pounds to be protected (as Actors) from a Law that has not since appeared to be against us.[2]

Elsewhere he describes even more explicitly the previous ambiguity in theatrical law.[3] Although his argument is poorly focused, his drift is clear enough: that the Licensing Act was desirable in so far as it removed confusion and consequent inequities.

To this legal argument he adds a prudential one: that the available supply of plays is not sufficient for more than two companies.[4] If additional theatres operated, he insists, there must be either excessive repetition or a resort to theatrical entertainments unworthy of public performance. Far from conceiving of theatrical competition as an incentive to excellence, he thought of it as a degrading force; and he would thus interpret the monopolistic aspect of the Licensing Act as a gain for audiences as well as for the patentees.

As for the censorship question, Cibber points out that Lord Chamberlains, whatever the legal basis of their authority, had often intervened in theatrical affairs, not only determining the outcome of theatrical revolutions, but sometimes forbidding performances of plays, even in instances when the Master of the Revels had granted a licence. The drift of his argument again

---

[1] *Apology*, i. 283. [2] Ibid. 284.
[3] Ibid. ii. 11. [4] Ibid. i. 297.

is clear: the Licensing Act regularized a power that previously had been exercised capriciously. 'By these Instances', he writes about episodes in which Lord Chamberlains had acted arbitrarily, 'we see how naturally Power only founded on Custom is apt, where the Law is silent, to run into Excesses, and while it laudably pretends to govern others, how hard it is to govern itself.'[1] Why, Cibber asks his opponents, are they so critical of a law which in essence defined an authority previously exercised without the support of law?[2]

Claiming to abhor any infringement upon the liberty of the press, he asserts his confidence that there is no such danger. A decisive difference separates licensing the press from licensing the stage, he argues, a difference that derives from the greater force of a dramatic over a printed libel. When a person reads a false or malicious libel, he may put it to the test of reason and knowledge and properly evaluate it; when in the theatre he sees and hears a libel supported by the talents of actors and the applause of fellow spectators, he finds himself swept to an uncritical acceptance of it, whatever the misrepresentation it may embody. The rhetorical strength of dramatic performances constitutes their danger in that reputations may be damaged beyond the possibility of amendment by subsequent punitive action. Cibber expresses the strongest revulsion against Fielding's dramatic caricature of Walpole:

> Was the Wound that *Guiscard* gave to the late Lord *Oxford*, when a Minister, a greater Injury than the Theatrical Insult which was offer'd to a later Minister, in a more valuable Part, his Character? Was it not as high time, then, to take this dangerous Weapon of mimical Insolence and Defamation out of the Hands of a mad Poet, as to wrest the Knife from the lifted Hand of a Murderer?[3]

Metaphorical frenzy leads to overstatement, but Cibber's point merits more consideration than it has been given.

Notwithstanding Cibber's opinion, it is hard to view the restriction of theatrical performances to the patent houses as other than a major misfortune to British drama. The old argument that fewer theatres competing for audiences would mean better plays and the encouragement of aspiring dramatists

---

[1] Ibid. ii. 22.   [2] Ibid. 23.   [3] Ibid. i. 291.

proved false. The patentees, their monopolies confirmed, were primarily interested in making a profit (just as their critics had for so long charged), and so continued to present plays of proved success and pantomimes sure to attract audiences. It is arguable, I have suggested, that the provision in the Licensing Act for limiting the number of theatres was more damaging than the provision for licensing plays.

The operation of the Act had a long and complex history; only the initial phase of that history, before it was amended and before political, social, and theatrical conditions were radically altered, concerns us here. What then was the immediate impact of the Licensing Act on English drama—and on English literature?

With respect to censorship, in the first years of the Act, only plays making the grossest kind of political allusion were banned. Two years passed before a play was prohibited by the Licenser, and that play, Brooke's *Gustavus Vasa*, was a political allegory in which both Walpole and the King himself are depicted in the guises respectively of a corrupt minister and foreign king tyrannically ruling an oppressed people, who are only nominally identified as Swedes.[1] In the same year a second play was prohibited, Thomson's *Edward and Eleonora*, and it, too, is a political piece that touches royalty. Based on a legend of Edward I, when he was Prince of Wales, the play is transparently a celebration of Prince Frederick;[2] and it contains an only slightly disguised appeal that he should supplant wicked Ministers in the councils of his father. Meanwhile, other plays hostile to Walpole were licensed and performed. Thomson's *Agamemnon* (1738), bolder than the subsequent *Edward and Eleonora*, has a dramatic situation based on Aeschylus' *Agamemnon* that would suggest the political situation: the working partnership of Queen Caroline

---

[1] Greene, *Politics of Samuel Johnson*, pp. 99–101.

[2] Grant, *James Thomson*, pp. 187–91. According to an implausible story in the *Biographia Dramatica* (1812; ii. 37), the fact that *Edward and Eleonora* was transcribed in the handwriting of Thomson's friend William Paterson led the Licenser in 1740 to refuse Paterson a licence for his own tragedy *Arminius*. Certainly the play was forbidden the stage. Yet if at this remove it seems politically innocent, it may not have been so in 1740. At any rate the character Segestes, the old leader who recommends an alliance with Rome (France?) and who urges the advantages which the surrender of freedom can bring, may stand for Walpole; whereas Arminius, the young patriot who recommends a noble defiance of tyranny, may stand for a leader of the opposition (cf. their debate in Act II).

and Walpole, who in the play are paralleled in the characters of Clytemnestra and Aegisthus.[1] Queen Caroline's death during the winter prior to the play's production removed its sting, and may have had something to do with the fact that it was licensed. Thomson's friend David Mallet also had a play of opposition temper licensed and performed; his *Mustapha* (February 1739) is a tragedy in which an evil minister alienates a prince and heir from his sovereign and father. The political application made the play, with the support of the opposition leaders, a resounding success;[2] and in fact it may have been this success which led the Lord Chamberlain and the Licenser to the greater caution evident in the prohibition of *Gustavus Vasa* and *Edward and Eleonora*.

Walpole apparently did not attempt to use the authority granted the Lord Chamberlain as a means to make the stage a vehicle for propagating ministerial opinion. Chesterfield's fears proved baseless in the event. Nor is there evidence that he attempted to stop the expression in drama of disagreement with his major policies. Thus the drama of the late 1730's, after the Licensing Act as well as before, rings with denunciations of Spain and appeals for an honourable war against her; this during the years when Walpole was trying to preserve the peace. Any form of censorship, we may agree with the spokesmen for the opposition, is regrettable; but this censorship seems to have been of a mild kind.

The enforcement of the patentees' monopolies was stricter, but it was not absolute. Fielding's company was, of course, promptly and permanently silenced. After an interval of several seasons, however, Giffard's was permitted to perform at Goodman's Fields under the most palpable of subterfuges—that of offering 'gratis' a comedy between the parts of a musical concert to which admission was charged.[3] As early as the autumn of 1738 a French company was licensed to perform in the Little Theatre in the Haymarket, but public indignation at the grant of a liberty to foreigners that was denied to Englishmen was such that the French performances were silenced by rioting.[4]

---

[1] Grant, *James Thomson*, pp. 178–86.   [2] Ibid., pp. 186–8.

[3] Scouten *London Stage*, I. lii–liii. See Scouten's account of the Licensing Act for an extended discussion of theatrical performances after 1737 apart from those in the patent houses.

[4] Cf. H. Walpole, *Memoirs of George II*, i. 14 n.

Theatrical performances elsewhere than at Drury Lane and Covent Garden were for many years irregular. Aspiring dramatists who wanted to have their plays performed well and profitably had to please the patentees; and this most of them found impossible to do.

Here is the most serious dramatic consequence of the Licensing Act: the limitation of the market available to playwrights. For a time in the 1730's, with four or five theatres operating, there seemed to be the promise of an exciting dramatic era[1]— of an escape from the doldrums that had stimulated the writers of dunciads. The multiplication of theatres meant that many more plays by new dramatists were given a chance; the trend of the past was in process of being reversed—when Walpole intervened. The patentees thereupon became dictators in earnest of English drama; and at least one of them, John Rich of Covent Garden, was grossly unfit for the responsibility. A pantomimist himself, reluctant to make additions to the repertory except in pantomime, he was the real villain of the mid-eighteenth-century theatres, the most unscrupulous profiteer from the monopolistic effect of the Licensing Act. Yet neither were the managers of Drury Lane very receptive to new plays.[2] In the theatrical situation that resulted from the Licensing Act may be found a reason for the growth of closet drama, and a reason too for the transfer of creative energy from the drama to the novel.

In fact, the most profound literary consequence of the Act may have been the impulse that it gave to the development of the novel. From the end of the seventeenth century there appears in drama what we may in retrospect call a novelistic drift, a movement away from formalization in plots, characterization, and dialogue toward a more complex and original treatment of them. We encounter characters in comedy— Worthy in Vanbrugh's *The Relapse*, for example, and Mirabell in Congreve's *The Way of the World*—who are too complex to be understood within the dramatic conventions of the Restoration tradition that was still dominant.[3] Mirabell, the dramatic character at the centre of the action, is an engaging fellow; and

---

[1] Cf. Scouten, *London Stage*, I. cxxxviii ff.

[2] Lynch, *Box, Pit and Gallery*, pp. 124–5.

[3] For suggestions on this subject, I am indebted to the late John Harrington Smith.

yet he appears in relationships—notably in those with Mrs. Fainall—which make it difficult for us to accept him as a sympathetic character. In brief, both Mirabell as a character and the dramatic action in which he is involved have a complexity which we are more likely to find in the subsequent novel than in the previous drama. Throughout the first four decades of the eighteenth century, drama (and especially comedy) moved progressively toward such complication, to the extent indeed that by the 1730's Fielding's *The Modern Husband* and William Popple's *The Lady's Revenge*, among other plays, seem to be dramatized novels.

They seem so, however, *in retrospect*, in the light of the development of the novel and the failure in the development of the drama. Had the Licensing Act not limited so severely the dramatists' opportunities to have their plays performed, had it not made experimentation in drama so difficult, might the drama itself not earlier have brought to artistic maturity some of the themes that we now call 'novelistic'? The question is a hypothetical one and cannot be answered. But the mediocrity of mid-eighteenth-century drama is well-documented fact, and we may plausibly attribute some responsibility for it to those who drafted the monopolistic provisions of the Licensing Act.

VII

CONCLUSION: THE POLITICAL STRAIN
IN AUGUSTAN DRAMA

APART from the governmental restrictions, there was nothing to prevent Augustan dramatists from turning satirical attention to political subjects, no inhibitory sense of propriety, such as kept religious subjects out of comedy if not out of tragedy. There was a relative freedom of expression, on the stage as in the press; there were well-defined and powerful opposing factions, numerically small and compact enough to be susceptible to adroit propaganda; and there was admiration for verbal ingenuity, even a willingness to examine it and applaud or damn it as deserved with a certain tolerance for difference of opinion. The age is remarkable for the political eminence enjoyed by literary men, just as it is remarkable for the literary eminence enjoyed by politicians, which is not the same thing. A political age, it produced a political drama—but a political drama that is clever rather than profound.

Wit there is in abundance, and adroit allusion to famous personalities; but not convincing treatment of the most important political relationships. The political themes are on the one hand narrowly partisan and on the other generalized to the point of being platitudinous. At the one extreme there is the personal allusiveness of *The Beggar's Opera*; at the other the oratorical dramatization of political theory in *Tamerlane*. The dramatists failed to express lively conflicts embodying rival political philosophies.

That they did not was in part owing to the nature of politics at the time. From a condition of opposition on fundamental issues, politics became progressively a matter of rivalries turning on personalities and the interests of fractions.[1] As early as the reign of Queen Anne, there were signs of weakening in the

---

[1] Cf. L. B. Namier's discussion of the absence of political issues in the mid-eighteenth century: *The Structure of Politics at the Accession of George III*, 2nd ed. (London, 1957), pp. 133–4; *England in the Age of the American Revolution* (London, 1930), pp. 206–7.

ideological differences between Tories and Whigs—as appears, among other ways, in the instance of the Tories' cheering *Cato*, and this at the height of their resurgence in the Queen's last years. The long ascendancy of Walpole encouraged an indifference to political ideas. In England, as in Lilliput, political principle became obscured by faction, and the English theatres produced the drama we would expect of Lilliput.

Political events, it will appear from the preceding chapters, caused changes in emphasis in both tragedy and comedy; but these changes came without much reference to distinctions between Whig and Tory. There is an emphasis in Restoration tragedy on the evils arising from disregard of the royal prerogative; an emphasis in tragedy produced after the Revolution on the evils arising from despotism. Dryden depicted the horrors of mob rule; Addison of tyrannical rule. *Cato* is the most famous instance in which a Roman points a political moral to the English, but there are many others, including the series of dramatizations of the heroic resistance made by Lucius Junius Brutus to the despotism of Tarquin. Tragedies celebrating the limitation of royal power, of constitutional monarchy as conceived by Locke, are abundant after the Revolution; tragedies celebrating the bounties that arise from the exercise of the royal prerogative or depicting the horrors that arise from the infringement of it are non-existent. Dramatists, to be sure, had a lively conception of the balance of powers as the foundation of English liberties; but they were far more sensitive to infringements on the powers of Lords and Commons than to infringements on those of the Sovereign. A dramatization of the history of the royal martyr Charles I appeared, but characteristically his impolitic and arbitrary acts are reprehended at the same time that his fate is deplored. It was William III, symbol of liberation from tyranny, who was the favoured hero of the dramatists. The absence of tragedies celebrating passive obedience and divine right provides a gauge of the intellectual bankruptcy of the older form of Toryism in the eighteenth century.

The social assumptions of Restoration comedy, which were related to political animosities, persisted long after the Revolution. Hatred of the dissenters as latter-day Puritans and of the business community which had supported Cromwell and

which in its bustling prosperity was a threat to aristocratic
privilege, this hatred determined the direction of satire in
comedy for some two decades after 1688, animating personal
rivalries depicted in the plays of, among others, Congreve,
Vanbrugh, and Farquhar. It is worth noting that these three
dramatists were Whigs, the two former indeed members of the
Whig Kit-Cat Club. The social attitudes that dominated
comedy until about 1710 (inherited, as I have said, from
Royalist attitudes of the Restoration) were then not held
merely by Tory reactionaries. Thereafter, with the parliamentary and journalistic debates that preceded and followed
the Treaty of Utrecht in 1713, Whig doctrine began to influence characterization, satire, and even in some comedies
pronouncements by normative characters. This is intermittent
in the second and third decades of the eighteenth century,
reversions to the older attitudes frequently occurring; but by
the fourth decade the new attitudes, which in origin certainly
were Whig, are so widespread in comedy that it would seem
gratuitous to associate them with the programme of any political
group. Just as before 1710 the attitudes that were Royalist
in origin are so widespread in comedy as not to admit of association with the Tory party, so after 1730 the new attitudes may
not properly be called Whig, even though they were Whiggish
in origin.[1]

It has been argued that sentimentalism, so prominent in
early eighteenth-century drama, is an expression of Whiggism.[2]
It would seem to me that we have overstated the differences
between Whigs and Tories on this as on other aesthetic subjects.
There are, of course, some affinities between the conception of
human nature responsible for sentimentalism and the theological liberalism we associate with Whiggism.[3] Sentimentalism
(which in its eighteenth-century sense I assume to be the interpretation of character, motive, and incident with reference to

---

[1] Loftis, *Comedy and Society from Congreve to Fielding, passim.*

[2] Cf. C. A. Moore, 'Whig Panegyric Verse, 1700–1760: A Phase of Sentimentalism', *PMLA*, xli (1926), 362–401.

[3] On the religious and intellectual background of sentimentalism, see Ronald
S. Crane, 'Suggestions toward a Genealogy of "The Man of Feeling"', *ELH,
A Journal of English Literary History*, i (1934), 205–30; Ernest L. Tuveson, 'The
Importance of Shaftesbury', ibid., xx (1953), 267–99; and Martin C. Battestin,
The Moral Basis of Fielding's Art (Middletown, Conn., 1959), Ch. V.

moral philosophy emphasizing innate benevolence[1]) is in its essential nature, with its glossing over of Original Sin and human depravity, incompatible with High Church orthodoxy and thus, logically at least, with Toryism. Swift, who represents so articulately the High Church mentality, expresses in his writings the very antithesis of the 'sentimental' assumption that men are fundamentally benevolent.[2] The single person most influential in bringing to focus moral philosophy with this emphasis was the third Earl of Shaftesbury, liberal in theological opinion to the point of deism, the grandson of the man usually described as the founder of the Whig party.

All this notwithstanding, sentimentalism was an aspect of ethical thought and Whiggism of political thought; and the two were quite distinct from one another. The reasons for conceiving of sentimentalism in drama as an expression of Whiggism will be seen to be ambiguous if we examine, not the logical implications of ideas, but the political activities and the plays of individual dramatists. I have mentioned Congreve, Vanbrugh, and Farquhar as Whig dramatists who preserved into the eighteenth century, or to the eve of it, the social attitudes of the Restoration. They were, at the same time, dramatists who resisted, and in the case of Vanbrugh satirized, the encroachments of sentimentalism. Vanbrugh's *The Relapse*, the sequel to Cibber's *Love's Last Shift*, is the most destructive of the contemporary critiques of dramatic sentimentalism; and it is destructive because of the honesty and audacity with which it examines the assumptions underlying Cibber's denouement. Since all the important dramatists who revealed political bias in Anne's and George I's reigns were Whigs, it is impossible to contrast attitudes toward sentimentalism expressed by adherents of the two parties. The Whig dramatists active during these reigns—Vanbrugh, Farquhar, Rowe, Steele, Mrs. Centlivre, Thomas Baker, William Burnaby, Charles Johnson, Addison, and Cibber (Whig at least after 1714)—included sentimental episodes in their plays so irregularly, if at all, that we can scarcely think of those episodes as a corollary

---

[1] For my conception of sentimentalism, see *Comedy and Society from Congreve to Fielding*, pp. 127–8.

[2] See Ernest L. Tuveson, 'Swift: The Dean as Satirist', *University of Toronto Quarterly*, xxii (1953), 368–75; and Roland Mushat Frye, 'Swift's Yahoo and the Christian Symbols for Sin', *Journal of the History of Ideas*, xv (1954), 201–17.

of their political affiliation. And the rout of the Tories was so complete after the accession of George I that they soon lost whatever cohesiveness as a political unit they had had. By the mid-1720's the significant political distinction was the one between the Walpole Whigs and the opposition.[1] Thus to associate sentimentalism with the Whig party of George I's and George II's reigns, without reference to the antagonism among Whigs between Court and Country parties, is to oversimplify; it is in fact to emphasize a political terminology which does not coincide with the political conditions of that time. Since most of those who were writing in the later years of George I and the earlier years of George II were Whigs, even if in opposition, it is easy to show that the expressions of sentimentalism (by Thomson, Dodsley, and Fielding, among many others) were by Whigs; but this seems to be little more than saying (what is undoubtedly true) that sentimentalism became pervasive in English literature at a time when the Whigs enjoyed an overwhelming ascendancy in English politics.

Like sentimentalism, neoclassicism would seem on first impression to be an aesthetic subject having political implications. There was a frequent metaphorical association of neoclassicism with France, which represented to the English both formalism in critical theory and absolutism in government. As early as Dryden's *Essay of Dramatic Poesy* some such association is implied,[2] and as late as Joseph Warton's *The Enthusiast* it is made epigrammatically.[3] French tyranny, even in art, and English freedom; these are contrasted, though not always in language carrying the same evaluations, through a century of English criticism. Often the contrast is described as being between French order and English anarchy (at least in art); but whatever the sympathies of the writer, the terms of the opposition remain fairly constant. The accomplishment of French seventeenth-century drama was such that English men of letters had to give respectful attention to it, whatever the conclusions they reached on the critical theory it embodied.

The metaphorical comparisons would suggest that the Tories,

---

[1] Realey, *Early Opposition to Sir Robert Walpole*, Ch. V; Feiling, *Second Tory Party*, Ch. II.

[2] Cf. *Essays of John Dryden*, ed. W. P. Ker (Oxford, 1900), i. 67–79.

[3] Ll. 25 ff. For further discussion of associations between political and critical theory, see Samuel Kliger, *The Goths in England* (Cambridge, Mass., 1952), pp. 3–6.

who were more sympathetic to absolutism in government and to the French than were the Whigs, would have been the more firm neoclassicists. Yet I see no evidence that this is true. The party affiliations did not noticeably affect dramatic criticism in its theoretical aspects. From the rough and tumble of party rivalries in the theatres, no clear, logical opposition of principles in dramatic theory emerges: the Tories did not as a group support classical regularity in drama, nor did the Whigs with any consistency oppose French tyranny in its dramatic application. Dennis, a strong Whig who wrote tragedies glorifying the Whig theory of government, was among the nation's firmest admirers of classical regularity in drama—of the 'tyranny' of French rules. He criticized the Whig Addison for his maladroit adherence to some of the rules and departure from others in *Cato*; and he roundly denounced the Whig Steele for his violation of the doctrine of kinds in *The Conscious Lovers*. Of the critical essays that Addison contributed to *The Spectator*, one famous group, on *Paradise Lost*, is neoclassical in assumptions and another famous group, on 'the pleasures of the imagination', is not at all, but rather provides a theoretical basis in aesthetics for much subsequent imaginative and critical writing in opposition to neoclassicism. Steele was inconsistent in his attitude toward the neoclassical rules, now observing them, now ignoring or even denouncing them. In short, Dennis, Addison, and Steele, all three of them Whig dramatists, disagreed as thoroughly on critical principles as they did on most other subjects except politics. And their disagreement illustrates a general absence of correlation between political and literary assumptions. To impose a pattern of association between political conviction and literary theory, with reference to support for or opposition to the doctrines of French formalism, is to inflate the importance of a metaphor beyond reasonable proportions and to ignore exceptions more important than the cases comprehended.

There are important correlations between the political and critical attitudes of the Augustan age, but they are fundamental ones which exist without much reference to the division between Whig and Tory. The body of common agreement, and of common change in both political and critical opinions with the passage of time, seems much more impressive than any critical

disagreements we may associate with partisan political affiliations. Attitudes toward the neoclassical doctrine of decorum
in characterization provide an instance of a parallel between
critical and political assumptions so fundamental as to have
little relevance to party differences. Dryden's and Rymer's
conceptions of propriety in characterization rest on assumptions
that are critical and political alike: that drama should imitate
the ideal order of society, conceived to be an hierarchical and
rather rigid structure. The later relaxation in the conceptions
of propriety evident in the eighteenth-century experiments in
domestic tragedy came from a weakening in the conviction
that drama should imitate an ideal order and from the social
dislocations accompanying the growth of the mercantile
community. The sympathetic hearing that Lillo's *The London
Merchant* received would have been impossible in Dryden's
time. Lillo, it is true, was a Whig, Dryden had been a Tory;
but the Whigs of Charles's reign no more held Lillo's critical
and political convictions than the Tories of the 1730's held
those of Dryden. The evidence in critical theory seems to me
to emphasize ideological affinities between Whigs and Tories
rather than differences.

The most obvious impact of politics on the drama is in the
practical area of propaganda. Effective propaganda must
be emphatic, and Augustan drama written in the service of
party or faction is emphatic indeed. The political motive led to
intensification, whether of tragic seriousness or of comic satire;
it led to the avoidance of ambiguity and even of subtlety.
Augustan tragedy is at best declamatory, and when the trage-
dians were at pains to make their plays point a political moral,
they made their characters mouth lectures of a preternatural
seriousness. We note and are repelled by an assurance of statement in Augustan tragedy, a positiveness that leaves little room
for the uncertainties that are so prominent in human experience
and hence in the greatest tragedies. To be sure, the propagandistic purpose was not the only reason, perhaps not even the
most important reason, for the declamatory tone and the
simplification of tragic issues. The Enlightenment was notoriously an age of intellectual self-confidence; and the Lockeian
political system that controlled tragedy after 1688 was a tidy
system, encouraging an intellectual tidiness in the plays. But it

seems clear enough that a propagandistic purpose led frequently to exaggerated earnestness, over-emphatic statement, and over-simplified argument. And this would seem to be a major reason why the plays are remarkable chiefly as a chronicle of their age.

INDEX

PRINTED IN GREAT BRITAIN
AT THE UNIVERSITY PRESS, OXFORD
BY VIVIAN RIDLER
PRINTER TO THE UNIVERSITY